Europe: Past, Present and Future

nova science publishers

www.novapublishers.com

Europe: Past, Present and Future

Genesis, Institutions, and Instruments of the European Union: A Concise Guide on Euro-Multilateralism
Anis Bajrektarevic (Author)
Nora Wolf (Author)
2022. ISBN: 978-1-68507-736-5 (Softcover)
2022. ISBN: 978-1-68507-852-2 (eBook)

The History of London
Walter Besant (Author)
2021. ISBN: 978-1-53619-867-6 (Hardcover)
2021. ISBN: 978-1-53619-974-1 (eBook)

A Walking Tour of Italy's WWII Battlefields: From the Salerno Landings to San Pietro Infine
Robert Irving Desourdis (Author)
Frank de Planta de Wildenberg (Author)
2021. ISBN: 978-1-53618-572-0 (Hardcover)
2021. ISBN: 978-1-53618-665-9 (eBook)

A Walking Tour of Italy's WWII Battlefields: Breaking the Gustav and Hitler Lines
Robert Irving Desourdis (Author)
Frank de Planta de Wildenberg (Author)
2021. ISBN: 978-1-53619-076-2 (Hardcover)
2021. ISBN: 978-1-53619-145-5 (eBook)

A Walking Tour of Italy's WWII Battlefields: From the Anzio Landings to Rome
Robert Irving Desourdis (Author)
Frank de Planta de Wildenberg (Author)
2021. ISBN: 978-1-53619-077-9 (Hardcover)
2021. ISBN: 978-1-53619-197-4 (eBook)

More information about this series can be found at https://novapublishers.com/product-category/series/europe-past-present-and-future/

Rebecca Dalli Gonzi,
Simon Grima
and Anthony Zarb Dimech

Construction Contracting in Malta during Wartime

Seeking Opportunities during a Time of Economic and Environmental Distress

nova
science publishers
www.novapublishers.com

DOI: https://doi.org/10.52305/CDOX8121

Library of Congress Cataloging-in-Publication Data

Names: Dalli Gonzi, Rebecca, author. | Grima, Simon, author. | Zarb-Dimech, Anthony, author.
Title: Construction contracting in Malta during wartime : seeking opportunities during a time of economic and environmental distress / Rebecca Dalli Gonzi, Simon Grima and Anthony Zarb Dimech.
Description: New York : Nova Science Publishers, [2022] | Series: Europe : past, present and future | Includes bibliographical references and index. |
Identifiers: LCCN 2022027434 (print) | LCCN 2022027435 (ebook) | ISBN 9781685078584 (paperback) | ISBN 9798886970104 (adobe pdf)
Subjects: LCSH: Construction industry--Malta--History--20th century. | World War, 1939-1945--Economic aspects--Malta. | Malta--Economic conditions--20th century.
Classification: LCC HD9715.M43 D35 2022 (print) | LCC HD9715.M43 (ebook) | DDC 338.4/7624094585--dc23/eng/20220706
LC record available at https://lccn.loc.gov/2022027434
LC ebook record available at https://lccn.loc.gov/2022027435

Published by Nova Science Publishers, Inc. † New York

Dedicated to all the people and families who lived and died during the war.

Contents

Preface

Risk is not a study limited to time.

The study of the effects of risk relates to the extension of time and the permutations and combinations of events in their progressive unravelling. The notion of modernity, an evolutionary justification for a turbulent array of hazards, drives rapid change, the majority of which is irreversible.

Wars bring about irreversible change, which has far-reaching consequences for future generations. We start to grasp the impact of these shifts as we experience them through time, and we research, write about, and learn from them.

Understanding the impact of post-war change requires contemplation. The aim to develop stronger post-war communities necessitates a reflection on how conflicts have separated mankind and how humanity's nature might be used to serve others. The plans that are made and the decisions taken, especially by those in positions of influence, carry greater weight in terms of the speed at which risks to humanity evolve if not addressed in time, along with their corresponding effects.

As we journey through age and experience our own wars, we can choose to blindfold our way through time or rise above with strength to reach out to others, a process which in truth brings about self-actualisation.

For those who choose to rise to the occasion, bravery is theirs to own.

Acknowledgements

We would like to thank Mrs Doriette Rizzo Naudi and her late Father the Late Magistrate Dr. Gawdenz Borg, who offered their assistance on behalf of their family and provided us with historical information and photos. Through their vivid recollections and descriptions, Chev. Angelo Grima and the family came 'alive'. A book without instilling a sense of emotion in the reader would be very pedantic indeed, and the stories and anecdotes provided enriched and enlivened the work. We would also like to thank all other members of family Grima for their assistance in providing photos and some clarification of facts.

We are happy and honoured that and the family agreed to help, and we are positively sure that it was no mere coincidence that the material regarding Chev. Angelo Grima and his firm passed along life's way. We believe it was God-incidence! May we honour the names of those who worked so hard for their family and country, emulate their examples and, in the process, add value to our history by putting their contribution for all to read. Our gratitude goes to Mr Simon Cusens and Mr Raymond Pantalleresco for making available documents and data to enrich this research.

The data collected has been made available thanks to the Grima family who originally resided in Zejtun, also in loving memory of the deceased members of the family. Mrs Doriette Rizzo-Naudi and her late father, Magistrate Gawdenz Borg, the main contributors of this book, were approached regarding the idea of writing about Chevalier Angelo Grima. They immediately accepted and offered their assistance on behalf of her family.

Chapter 1

Financial Contracting

Financial structure decisions have evolved, from treating profitability as given, acknowledging that human actions affect profitability, and recognising that value depends on the allocation of decisions or control. In this book, we argue that the decision or control approach is useful, even though it is at an early stage of development and that the approach has some empirical content. It can shed light on the structure of capital contracts and the reasons for the diversity of objectives (Grima et al., 2021).

"Financial Contracting", as defined by Hart (2001), is the theory of deals that are carried out between financiers and those who need financing, or as we see it, those who come up with innovative ideas and can bring together the demand and supply to the benefit of multiple parties. That is those who determine a 'win-win' deal for all parties.

To motivate further, we ask the question: Suppose in a time of distress, high unemployment, hunger, no money, and low morale, opportunities open up. What does it take to identify them and act on them? How are opportunities realised? How did they get off the ground and source finance?

Although questions like these have been the focus of corporate finance and financial management studies and literature, as far as we understand, none of these studies focussed on case studies of the development of Maltese construction contracting during wartime, specifically during World War II between 1940 and 1945.

Therefore, we plan to carry out a historical review of the development of construction contracting in Malta during wartime by delving into the social needs, the environment, and the main characters' profiles together with the background and drive these people had to identify and seek opportunities and see them through.

Why a Maltese Case Study?

Malta is a small European island state situated in the centre of the Mediterranean. It has a population of circa 450,000 inhabitants, with native

Maltese comprising the vast majority of its inhabitants. Malta covers just over 316 km^2, is a full member of the European Union (EU) and forms part of the Eurozone. There are some very specific aspects of Malta's history that contribute to this study's interesting features (Grima et al., 2020).

Malta's governmental and administrative structure is similar to that of Great Britain in many ways. In a sense, this is an inevitable consequence of Malta having been a British Crown Colony between 1800 and 1964, after which Malta became independent. Studies have shown that colonies of the British Empire are more democratic than other colonies (Anckar, 2004; Samy et al., 2008). Unlike several other small island states, Malta has strong and diverse political parties, a centralized system of government but with a local council system, and a national Constitution that provides for the required existence of a number of scrutinising agencies and a rigid system of legal checks and balances (Pirotta, 2001). Furthermore, Malta has political and economic stability, and Worldwide Governance Indicators (The World Bank, 2013) rated Malta highly in all six broad aspects of governance (Kaufmann et al., 2010) (Bezzina et al., 2014).

With the provisions of the Treaty of Paris in 1814, the British gained full sovereignty of the Maltese Islands, which became a strategic and important part of the British Empire. The British could thereby expand their strategic stronghold in the Eastern region and the Mediterranean Sea. They reconfirmed Malta as a strategic military base in the centre of the Mediterranean. They added more forts and changed the fortification system previously built by the Knights of Saint John. The main constructions were military villages with barracks, parade grounds, hospitals and schools, some of which, although put to different use, are still being used to this date.

Moreover, Malta's ports and airstrips were strategically important for the British navy and the Royal Air Force (RAF), who continued to maintain and build ships, develop and maintain several airstrips. Malta was very simply considered a large military base, which was heavily bombarded in the 2nd world war and most of Malta's heritage was destroyed and replaced by military installations.

This important link was never more evident than during World War II when the Maltese islands played a crucial role "in the Mediterranean theatre of war, as a supply station and as a base for the recovery of the injured during the 1st world war (earning the Islands' title, 'Nurse of the Mediterranean')." In fact, King George V acknowledged the bravery of the Maltese people during World War II by awarding them his George Cross for valour (Bondin, 2014).

Malta during World War II

Malta was, at the time, the only Allied base between Gibraltar and Alexandria, Egypt. It was a station for the British trade route to Egypt and the Suez Canal to India and the Far East.

Hence Malta was considered by the allies as a strategically important island in the Mediterranean Sea during World War II. Malta pitted the navies and air forces of the German Nazis and the Italian Fascists against the British Royal Navy and Air Force (RAF). Malta played a major role in the eventual Allied success in North Africa. It was considered by the British prime minister, an “unsinkable aircraft carrier” (Boustany, 2001), which ensured that enemy ships transported vital supplies and reinforcements from Europe to Axis forces in North Africa. In fact, he highlighted that “without Malta, the Axis will end by losing control of North Africa”.

The strategic importance of the Island soon attracted the attention of the Axis forces, who bombed Malta heavily to starve the Island into submission, by constant attacks on the ports, towns and cities. They dropped more than 6,700 tons of bombs on the inner harbour alone.

Serving as the base that concerted assault by the RAF and their Fleet Air Arm aircraft, and Royal Navy submarines, on Axis supply lines across the Mediterranean from Italy to North Africa meant that there was a constant need for fast construction to create a sophisticated defence system at land, air and sea.

Malta was an easy target and a far cry from having a sophisticated defence system from the air. The three airfields and the Grand harbour were the four military targets, all confined in a small area in the south of the Island. The condition of the airfields was poor, with narrow strips limited by rocky outcrops and ravines; one of them was dominated by hills on three sides and built on a grass surface that bogged easily.

Furthermore, an average of 5,524 private houses were destroyed and 9,925 were damaged but repairable, on this heavily populated island. A total of 30,000 structures were destroyed or damaged, including 111 churches, 50 hospitals, schools or colleges, 36 theatres, clubs, government offices, banks, industries, wheat mills, and other commercial facilities (Spooner, 1996). Among these, The Royal Opera House, Auberge d’Auvergne, Auberge de France and Palazzo Correa in Valletta, the Birgu Clock Tower, Auberge d’Allemagne and Auberge d’Italie in Birgu, parts of the fortifications of Senglea, and the Governor’s House of Fort Ricasoli were destroyed. Other buildings such as Auberge de Castille, Auberge de Bavière, the Casa del

Commun Tesoro and parts of Fort Manoel also suffered extensive damage but were rebuilt after the war.

Source: Russell, J.E. (Lt) (n.d.) *Extensive bomb damage in Valletta, 1942*. Available at: http://media.iwm.org.uk/iwm/mediaLib//29/media-29365/large.jpg.

Figure 1. Extensive bomb damage in Valletta, 1942. The Royal Theatre is on the right.

Ensuring Sustainability in a Time of Distress

Sustainability is characterised by the need to balance societal needs, the economy, and the environment, which are not mutually exclusive but interrelated and linked with one another. Determining opportunities requires that one proactively and continuously identifies the risk (in this case, defined as the variance from the expected or the norm) and addresses it continuously and sustainably (Grima, 2021).

In truth, the story of life and progress is about managing these risks (i.e., risk management) by detecting risk (i.e., opportunities and threats) and deciding whether to move them away entirely or partially to those who can handle them better or find ways to address them. However, to be successful and maintain continuity, one must always consider societal demands, the environment and economic needs. Some might agree that the most important needs are emergency shelters, rural reconstruction, and refugee returnee post-war programs. These are, of course, important; however, they only cater for the immediate assistance that alone is not sufficient for sustainability. Sustainability is not only about the ability to balance the three pillars (environment, social needs, economy) in an available scenario, but ensuring that this does not compromise the ability of future scenarios and needs (Clark, 2008). In this regard, there is an ever-growing need for individuals to determine the context in which a country's economic activity takes place (Zarb -Dimech, 2002).

Determinants of Opportunities during a War

An important necessity for a nations' prosperity is knowledge and perception of sound investment opportunities. However, the extent and nature of opportunities are not easy to discover, especially since they change with the many fluctuating relationships and vary with anticipations and perceptions, which determine social needs. War is one of the catastrophic forms of variance from the norm and, therefore, risk, and it alters, at least for a time, all major social and economic relationships. To a large extent, it complicates the forecasting and expectations and hence appraisals.

However, case studies can enable us to determine and generalise what types of influences have been critical in distressed situations and direct our attention to those factors, which are universal.

One of the prerequisites of opportunity seekers is the willingness to change and challenge the status quo. This attitude makes them willing to undertake challenges with determination and energy. However, this as some would assume, is not always instigated by greed for money or addiction, but a result of vision and ability to manage the uncertainty in the economic and social security and stability during the period (Dulles, 1942).

Our approach, therefore, is to build the picture in the next few chapters to expose the main characters involved in the construction industry, the environment and the social needs. We approach this by carrying out a systematic review of literature available or gathered from families and by listening and transcribing some of the stories related by family descendants. These structured stories about personal experiences and narratives were used to understand the past, construct identities, and communicate this to others. Drawing on social literature on narratives, identities, and autobiographical memories, this study examines the contracting construction industry, recitation, and evaluation of World War II narratives. We aim to construct the influential factors that empower people to seek opportunities and delve where others would not dream to. We are particularly interested in the ways they constructed meanings about their experiences and the ways they constructed their identities in relation to those experiences.

However, one must keep in mind that people tell stories for a variety of reasons. The storyteller presents some kind of purpose or intention in a narrative form, usually tailored to a particular audience. Moreover, cultural norms, values, and traditions influence their stories and tell the how, when, and why. The one passing on the story might determine tales that are not worth telling and particularly privilege stories over others (Wiest, 2013).

Chapter 2

The Characters

The Main Character in Construction Contracting during World War II

The main character in this book, Chevalier Angelo Grima, is the key to much of the information about contracts in the 1900s. Chev. Angelo Grima used to be continually aided and supported in his construction contracting profession by two of his brothers, Carmelo and Joseph Grima. The diagram below depicts the family tree.

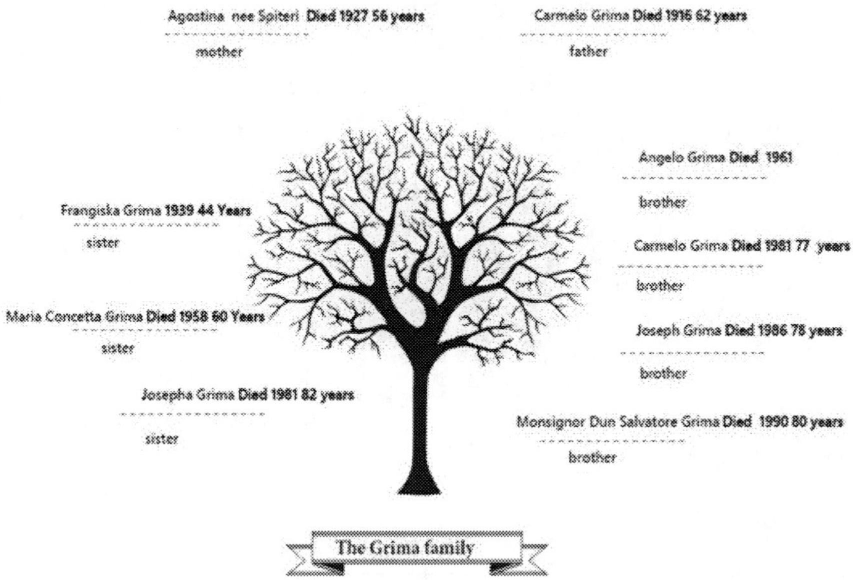

Source: Authors' Compilation.

Figure 2. The Grima Family Tree.

Every town and hamlet in Malta can boast of its sons and daughters who have made Malta proud. Zejtun is no different. In the Maltese town of Zejtun, Chevalier Angelo Grima, or 'Is-Sur Gulin tal-Qutu' (the latter being the family nickname), is a remarkable example. Chevalier Angelo Grima was a single man with a small and short build, a blond complexion, and white, thick hair. He was a man with a strong personality and a keen intellect. He enjoyed his drink and as he would say, it aided him in socializing. Above all, 'Gulin' was a reliable businessman with a giving heart who valued doing the right thing. Money did not control him despite his financial stability. Chevalier Angelo Grima was born in Zejtun in 1893, the firstborn of seven siblings to Carmelo Grima (Senior) and Agostina nee' Spiteri. He graduated from a Government Elementary School at the young age of 13. In front of the Zejtun Parish Church, his father had hired a coffee shop (In its place now stands a bank). Together with his sister Cikka, Gulin assisted at his father's store (Zarb Dimech, 2010).

Top left to right - Frangiska, Carmelo and his wife, Emmanuela.
Bottom Left to the right – Josepha, Angelo and Maria Concetta.
Their Brothers Joseph and his wife Maria Stella and Salvatore are not in this photo.
Source: Authors' Compilation.

Figure 3. Family Photo.

Customers sometimes told Carmelo (Senior) that Gulin was more of a man than a youngster. Carmelo died at a young age, and Gulin and Cikka took over the shop's management. The shop thrived under their leadership, but not long after Carmelo's demise, Cikka died. Gulin was now in charge of the store. He would open the shop in the early morning hours, around 3.30 a.m., when the coal miners went out for coffee. Several jobless men who had also come for coffee soon joined them. . Gulin may recall a hefty gentleman with two young sons who visited the establishment. They would bring bread slices to dip in their coffee and consume with it. This was the level of poverty in Zejtun. Gulin would empathize with them when their cups were empty and offered additional coffee. These three men would gather the horses' faeces keeping it in their back yards, and, eventually selling it to farmers as fertilizer (Zarb Dimech, 2010).

Source: Authors' Compilation.

Figure 4. Angelo's brother Carmelo Grima.

Source: Authors' Compilation.

Figure 5. Angelo's brother Joseph Grima (senior).

The majority of Gulin's coffee shop clients were males who, although the primary breadwinners, were unemployed. Gulin learnt that the government was awarding a contract for trenching employees to carry out a job between

'Bir-id-Deheb' to 'Zejtun' Square through a tender process. He took the initiative and asked his unemployed clients if they would be interested in working for him if he were to tender for the job. They were all ecstatic to hear the news and gladly accepted it. Following that, Gulin was awarded the contract, and all of these men worked and earned their wages, with profit left over for Gulin. This was the beginning of Gulin's career as a construction contractor. He was able to win several contracts and hire many employees, even from the outskirts of Zejtun.

Prior to World War II, he was granted the contract for building the Luqa airfield, which was his greatest work contract. To carry the materials needed for construction, Gulin used many horse-drawn carts. Here, he developed a passion for horses (Zarb Dimech, 2010).

Gulin would talk about his regular travels to the Augustinian Convent in Valletta's Strada Forni (now Old Bakery Street), where he would pray for Saint Rita's intercession, of whom he was a devout follower. He claims that these prayers provided him with great insight and direction. Gulin eventually bought the coffee shop and the other little cottages in front of the Church. He merged the properties and invited his father's family to relocate from the village's lower section and make this new house theirs. Agostina, his mother, and Cikka, his sister, both died at these homes.

Giuseppina, who was unmarried, baked pastries for the coffee shop. He would provide the pastries to the locals who came to his coffee shop whenever he could get some work from contractors. Local men would come to his café, and Gulin began to profit from this. Strong men who were jobless would come to the business, but when Gulin learned that a local contractor needed some labourers, he would give it to the men who came to his coffee shop. When a job contract arrived, he calculated how many people would be needed and filled the contract's paperwork.

After making a profit on his first contract, he was encouraged to take on a second one. He liked talking to people and getting to know them and he was a prayerful man who recited his prayers regularly. Before applying for a government contract, he would pray in front of the Saint Rita statue, asking for advice on whether he should increase or lower the amount of the offer he was making, and the government would accept the lowest bid, as was customary. Thus he began to win more contracts. He would then engage jobless persons sitting in his coffee shop and provide them with work opportunities (Zarb Dimech, 2010).

Angelo was bestowed the title of Chevalier by the Knights of Saint George, and there is a painting of Angelo dressed as a Chevalier in the sacristy of the parish church in Zejtun. Gulin and his other sister, Concetta, raised their siblings together. This is why Gulin never married, despite the fact that he always maintained that he would have liked to marry and raise a family of his own but could not afford it since it would have interfered with his obligations to his younger siblings.

Source: Authors' Compilation.

Figure 6. Chevalier Angelo Grima (3rd from right in the first picture and standing 4th from the right in the 2nd picture) at the inauguration of the Malta Airlines.

Angelo was a nice man who was always prepared to assist those in need. He liberally contributed his money, and one of his most worthwhile projects was the establishment of 'Id-Dar tal-Kleru' in Birkirkara (a house for priests past their prime), which is still operational today. In addition, he would make daily sacks of food for the beggars that swarmed Zejtun at the time. His weekly shopping cost was believed to be about Lm400 (932 Euro in today's money), indicating the amount of charity he used to engage in. He stated that God had been good to him and that it was his responsibility to repay him. His precise words were, 'Min jiekol waħdu, jixraq waħdu' ('He, who eats alone, coughs alone').

He also paid for the 'dota' (dowry) and education of many destitute Zejtun females and lads. Chev. Angelo Grima was also very covert in his charitable activities, and he would occasionally agonize over what he had donated, fearful of offending the individual. Mrs Doriette Rizzo-Naudi (his brother Joseph's first granddaughter) told us that when she was born, her parents celebrated her baptism at home and had London Confectionery (previously situated in Floriana) cater for the festivities. Her Uncle Gulin, true to his personality hurried to the confectionary and paid the bill before her father had an opportunity to do so. He was in misery for days, wondering if he had insulted Doriette's father (The Late Magistrate Dr Gawdenz Borg) by denying him the pleasure of paying for his own child's birthday celebration. He finally confessed everything to her grandfather (Joseph Grima), crying and pleading with him to tell her father what he had done and ask forgiveness on his behalf. Gulin had been a nervous mess when her parents went to thank him for his thoughtful gesture.

Doriette's parents were obviously overjoyed by this thoughtful gesture, which perhaps explains why her younger sister followed shortly afterwards. His generosity was not limited to monetary donations. Ms Rizzo-Naudi recalls Gulin slowly pouring Doriette's Sunday soup into a battered plastic dish she favoured and spoon-feeding her while reciting imaginative stories about stars and galaxies until she completed her portion of soup (Zarb Dimech, 2010).

He developed a love for the odd tot or two later in life. He never went too far, and he was never caught inebriated. Professor Craig, his doctor, advised him to limit his alcohol use and limited him to "social drinking." Gulin would wait outside his house, wanting to obey his doctor's directions but not willing to give up alcohol, and invited everybody passing by (even the postman and the dustman) in for a drink. In this case, Professor Craig meant "social drinking," he said.

According to the late retired Magistrate Dr Gawdenz Borg, son in Law of Joseph Grima (Angelo's brother), Angelo had two mottos: 'tiekolx whadek ghax tixraq wahdek', which meant 'do not eat on your own (or venture on your own) because you risk choking alone (you risk struggling on your own'), and 'titkabbarx u toghlewx ghax meta tasal il-gurnata tat-tisbita ahjar taqa' mil-baxx; which meant 'do not gloat and think highly of yourself because when the day of humiliation comes, it would be wiser to fall from a low stool than a high one'.

When the Second World War came, his business had grown, and he had employed almost half of the Zejtun village. That was his life target. He could not stand seeing people at the time who suffered from hunger because they had no work. So, he bought a wheelbarrow and started preparing for small contracts. He would make friends quickly, and he was very altruistic. He managed to penetrate the British high class and started his life out as a socialist. He knew how to complement others, and he was a very likeable and religious person.

In the meantime, he educated his siblings well, even though he did not attend secondary school himself. He thought he could take risks and be at the forefront of dangerous ventures after he knew the younger ones had a decent education and were settled. He would also carry a Santa Rita dedication to protect him and his workers, particularly when stationed around the runway. The story goes on to say that Saint Rita spoke to him through his brothers and said that she wanted to dedicate a home for retired priests. He designed and built the Dar tal-Kleru as a retirement home for priests to express gratitude for all of the safety they were afforded during the conflict (Zarb Dimech, 2010).

The war finished, and Angelo became a very wealthy man. He fostered a healthy and wealthy empire, which would eventually include the setting up of Malta's first airline in 1947 - Malta Airlines. He had the vision that he needed to start a business of passenger aeroplanes and started the airline as the major shareholder. Malta airlines then became Air Malta. The old airport was his property as a shareholder. He semi-retired and employed his younger siblings (Carmelo Junior. and Joseph) to take over the management.

He had won a number of contracts and had a lot of skilled men working for him as a contractor, erecting structures as part of his team. The English Military service that was the main employer had appointed Angelo as the contactor of the airport project. He worked on Malta's first small airport, and since he was now being recognised as a business entrepreneur, he was winning many contracts. As soon as a work contract was issued publicly, The English Military would want to assign the work directly to him. He made a lot of money and bought many properties. Since he took on many building construction projects, their house was always filled with British guests.

In fact, the military trusted him, and when war broke out, he made acquaintances with many high-ranking military officials. He employed people from 'Had Dingli' – they would arrive at Zejtun and from there go to different places. 'Serafin Xuereb' and 'Angelo' were the main contractors at the time.

In January 1941, following attacks on the airport built by Angelo, he had a contract from the Royal Air-force to fill in holes from bombs, so the airport could function since planes could not land and fly back up.

Additionally, Angelo took over a quarry in Marsascala to cut stone. He put his brother Carmelo (Junior)., also known as the 'Foreman' to take charge of onsite work, and stone from the quarry at 'Sant Antnin' in Marsascala where they had a crusher to break stones and make even smaller stones (żrar). The broken stones were used at the airport to fill in the holes. They would fill boxes and continue the process.

Angelo had two small trucks and one large truck, and they filled it with 'xaħx' during the night. During the day, they would fill the holes. They would conceal beneath trees with a horse and carriage and laborers, and when the German bombers had dropped bombs and left, the workmen would emerge from the woods and fill in the runway holes. One hole took up approximately two boxes full of stones and was topped up with sand. The asphalt was put on the top, and a roller was passed onto the filling. They managed to fill all the holes on the runway, and workers would work concurrently. It was a very dangerous contract, and he made a vow to build a small church dedicated to Saint Rita if they were kept safe. When they finished the filling, they would make sure the runway was serviceable again. Then another air raid would follow, and the process would repeat. Every barrel that was emptied would return to Marsascala for refilling.

The airport kept its operations because he did a lot of work. He made a lot of money because the Air-force paid him well. Angelo maintained good relations with English authorities and made good connections. He would pray to Saint Rita about the contracts he would acquire.

Angelo put his other brother Joseph in charge of the paperwork, administration and office duties, which he took care of from the offices and huts in 'Wied Dalam'.

Id- Dar tal Kleru (Christus Sacerdos) - The Home for the Clergy

Angelo's labour did not end there or with him; his siblings Carmelo, Joseph, and Salvatore continued it. In fact, Angelo helped finance his youngest brother's (aged 19 years) preparation to become a priest. Salvatore, or Salvu as his siblings called him, went on to study philosophy and theology at the Scottish college in Rome, a Gregorian University. On the 23rd December 1933, he was ordained as a priest in the Chapel of the Benedict sisters in Mdina and his first mass was celebrated in the Zejtun Parish Church dedicated to St. Catherine. He was known as Dun Salv.

Source: Author's Compilation.

Figure 7. Monsignor Prof. Dun Salvatore Grima.

He continued his studies and achieved a doctorate in Philosophy in 1930 and a doctorate in theology in 1936 from the Pontifical Scots College in Rome, a Gregorian University. He then started to teach religion at the seminary in Malta, and in 1937 he became the vice-rector.

During the scholastic year 1938-1939, Dun Salv attended courses at Kind's College in London and in October 1939, he became a Professor in Logic and Philosophy at the Royal University of Malta. He occupied this post between 1939 and 1949. In 1949, Dun Salv decided to give up teaching to dedicate himself more fully to a life of service among his brother priests.

Dun Salv asked his brothers to help him satisfy his wish to build a resting home for elderly priests, who found themselves alone after a life of service to the people and God. Angelo and his brothers accepted immediately. He also found the full support of Sir Michael Count Gonzi, the Roman Catholic Archbishop of Malta to find the necessary land. By the 1940s, about 24 acres of land within the confines of Fleur-de-Lys and Birkirkara, which belonged to the Cathedral Chapter, was in the hands of Dr Guizeppi Pace with an emphyteusis for 100 years. In 1948, Dr Pace agreed to give up his remaining 68-year emphyteusis to enable the construction of the 'Dar tal-Kleru (Christus Sacerdos)' a resting home for the elderly priests. With the constant help of his brothers (Angelo, Carmelo Jnr. and Joseph), Dun Salv embarked on this project, which was completed and started to operate on the 8th May 1964. Unfortunately, Angelo passed away in 1961 before its completion.

Source: Louis Cardona Melitensia Collector (Source of photo unknown).

Figure 8. The Home for the Clergy, Fleur De Lys, Malta.

Source: Author's compilation.

Figure 9. Archbishop Michael Gonzi at St. Paul's Cathedral, Mdina, Malta.

Following Angelo's death, the building was resumed from 'Wied Dalam' by his brothers Carmelo Jr. and Joseph, as well as several of their sons, over the following few years. In the 1980s, however, they altogether quit.

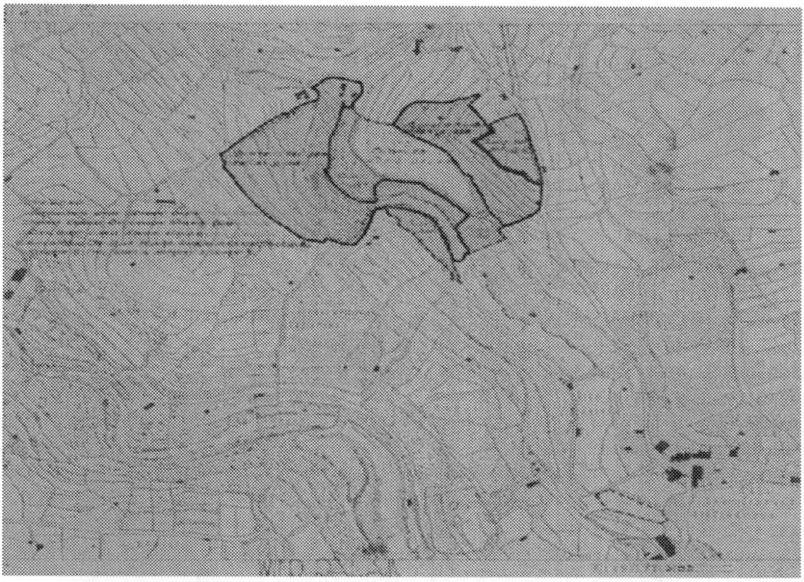

Source: The National Archives of Malta (n.d.). *Wied Dalam.* [ONLINE] Available at https://arkivji.org.mt/share/Plans/PDM61411.jpg [Accessed 01 January 2022].

Figure 10. Wied Dalam.

Chapter 3

Malta: A Contextual Background

Social and cultural factors will give the reader a glimpse of Malta and the Maltese during the decade preceding the start of the Second World War. As change occurred and Malta progressed through several stages, growth continued, and new influences and norms aided in developing successful results.

Historical Background

The Maltese population had grown from 213,395 in 1911 to 241,621 in 1931. Malta was densely populated for an island 17 miles long and 8 miles wide. The Maltese were a mixed-race but predominantly Latin. Maltese people are somewhat good-looking, with men being sturdily built and of average stature, while the women, with their dark hair and flashing eyes, have much in common with those of Southern Italy.

During this period, most of the population lived in Valletta and the harbour region and depended upon the naval and military establishments for their livelihood. The second-largest source of employment was agriculture. About seven-tenths of the land surface was cultivated, mostly in three or four acres holdings.

To economise the land better, dwellings were concentrated in large villages on barren ground and watered from rain tanks, deep wells, or springs along the blue clay's outcrops that separate the upper from the lower limestone. For cultivation, the light dusty soil was concentrated by terracing and protected against dry winds by high walls and irrigated from wells, as there are no perennial streams.

During this period, the picturesque costume formerly worn by Maltese men, now seldom seen, consisted of a cotton shirt, full trousers held by a girdle, a large waistcoat with ornamental buttons, a very short cloak and a coloured cap. The women, too, had changed their costume, although women of all classes outdoors still commonly wore the black Faldetta. It was a loose cloak covering the whole figure and gathered, as its name implies, into a stiff hood worn on one side of the face as a screen against passers-by.

Successive constitutions were enacted and developed, combining military administration of the Maltese Fortress with the legislature and judicature of a Crown Colony. All these Constitutions had developed defects in administering a population of around 250,000 dependent for their income on a naval base maintained for necessary purposes distinct from local needs. The implications of the emerging demographic and economic trends during this period were far-reaching, with emigration being resorted to as an official tool for population control. The effects of emigration created imbalances of sexes of marrying age within the Maltese population. The female population grew faster than the male population leading to an increase in the number of mixed marriages as the Maltese female had a lesser possibility of marrying a Maltese male.

The years between 1939 and 1945 brought about much suffering and death not only worldwide but also to the people of the Maltese Islands. The consequences of war were to be felt for several years after the war ended. The cruel siege on Malta between 1940 and 1943 brought about hunger, fear, death, and destruction. As noted in the first chapter, houses were destroyed, and the population sought refuge far away from its hometown or village and in shelters to avoid the cruel and savage air bombardment. More than 1,495 civilians lost their lives, and six times as many servicemen lost their lives in the battle for Malta.

When the war started, there were very few shelters.

> "People were advised to seek refuge in any safe place such as their basements, under the stairs or even beneath sturdy tables cushioned with layers of mattresses. As the war intensified, the excavation of rock-cut shelters gained momentum, and by June 1941, there were 473 public rock shelters with a further 382 under construction, protecting 138,000 people. Thousands more also sought refuge in concrete or private shelters" (Bishop, n.d.).

Later, women and children were permitted to excavate private cubicles within public shelters.

> "The air was filled with the crash of masonry and the uncanny swirl of blast. The building above was hit. Clouds of dust penetrated the shelter, smothering and half-choking the shelterers with dust, mostly women with babies and young children. Some children were terrified and cried, but their mothers, open-eyed and stupefied, calmly dipped their

handkerchiefs in a pail of water kept in the shelter for the purpose and put them over the mouths and noses of the babies. Then hugging their youngest to their bosom, they muttered a silent prayer." Foreign Correspondent, Reuters 1942 (Bishop, n.d.)

Source: Bishop, A. (n.d.) *Underground life during the war: Malta's air-raid shelters. [ONLINE]* Available at: https://www.guidememalta.com/en/underground-life-during-the-war-malta-s-air-raid-shelters [Accessed 01 January 2022].

Figure 11. Maltese Women with Faldetta.

Source: Bishop, A. (n.d.) *Underground life during the war: Malta's air-raid shelters. [ONLINE]* Available at: https://www.guidememalta.com/en/underground-life-during-the-war-malta-s-air-raid-shelters [Accessed 01 January 2022].

Figure 12. Underground air raid shelters.

Source: Bishop, A. (n.d.) *Shelters. [ONLINE]* Available at: https://www.guidememalta.com/en/underground-life-during-the-war-malta-s-air-raid-shelters [Accessed 01 January 2022].

Figure 13. Shelters.

British Military Fortifications

The two-year French occupation of Malta (1798-1900) ended on 5 September 1800, marking the beginning of the British colonial period. The first step taken by the British Military authorities was to maintain the bastion walls. Another aspect of the defence was the defence of St. Paul's and Marsaxlokk bays, considering that the strong French fleet was still present.

The British also completed many fortifications and bastions left incomplete from the Knights era. One of these projects was the Santa Margarita Lines and the Cottonera Lines. Some bastion walls had to be changed to accommodate new British artillery.

The Drydocks at the Grand Harbour had top priority because it was here that the Naval Fleet was serviced. In 1840, the British military authorities were advised to build a defensive line between the Kottonera and Santa Margarita lines. The British took this advice on board, and the St. Clement defensive line and Fort Verdala were constructed as well as Fort Lascaris under the Upper Barakka to defend the Drydocks and the inner part of the Grand Harbour in the event of an enemy ship entering the harbour.

Alterations were also made to existing Forts such as Fort St. Elmo, Fort Ricasoli, Fort Tigne', Fort Manoel and Fort St Angelo. These were some of the major works undertaken during the 19th Century.

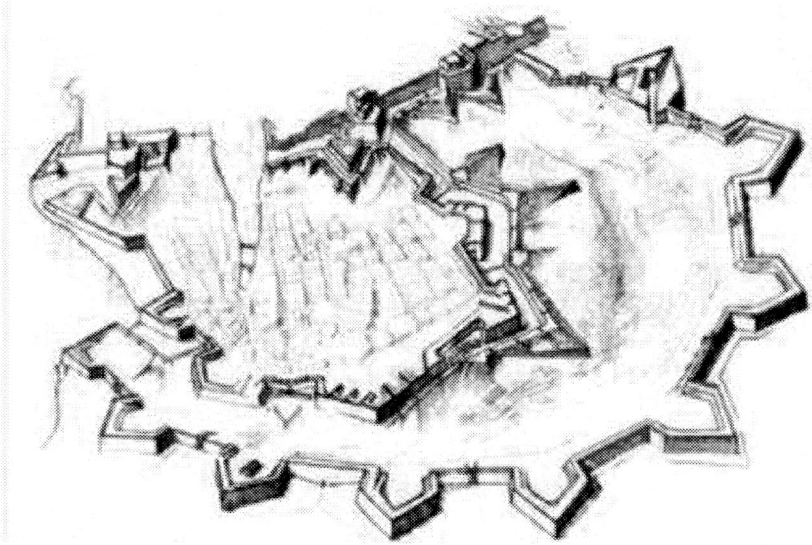

Source: Malta360. (year unknown) *Map of the Cottonera and Santa Margherita Lines.* [ONLINE] Available at: https://maltain360.com/default.aspx [Accessed 01 January 2022].

Figure 14. Map of the Cottonera and Santa Margherita Lines.

Source: Mizzi J.A., Vella M.A. (2001) *Malta at War.* Malta: Wise Owl.

Figure 15. The armed trawler HMS Coral within a bomb-damaged Dry Dock No. 3 during World War II.

The development of other bases did not diminish Malta's value. The port of Aden was acquired in 1839, Cyprus was leased from the Turks in 1878, and Egypt was occupied in 1882 - all of which became links in a chain of imperial stations, that stretched from the United Kingdom through Gibraltar, the Mediterranean and the Red Sea to India, the Straits and Singapore. Eventually, the chain of command and communications served the stations on the Chinese coast, Australia, and New Zealand. Malta was a hinge point in the imperial system. It was the headquarters of the Mediterranean fleet and secured a seaway vital to British interests (Blouet, 2004).

During the 20th Century, the British continued to build defensive batteries, such as in Gharghur (1900), Pembroke (1909-12), Tal-Wardija (1915-16), and Fort Benghisa (1910). Malta was very well defended during the First World War, and no attack by enemy forces occurred.

During the Second World War, the war strategies changed with the developments and advancements in aviation technology, and Malta was now within reach of any threat implying the need for better protection against aerial attacks. For this purpose, the batteries at Pembroke and Tal-Wardija were closed as they were considered obsolete. Due to this change in strategic aerial warfare, the shift was on beachhead protection such as beach posts and pill-boxes, anti-aircraft batteries, and underground installations to protect important stations such as communications and personnel.

Year	Fleet Personnel			Ships in Fleet				Dockyard Industrial Employees
	Officers	Men	Total	Large	Medium	Small	Total	
1879	450	6,300	6,750	4	3	15	22	
1884	452	6,328	6,780	6	2	14	23	
1889	341	4,774	5,115	3	4	13	20	
1894	633	8,862	9,495	11	7	12	30	
1899	833	11,662	12,495	10	10	21	41	3,334
1904	1,233	15,862	16,095	12	16	31	59	5,095
1909	563	7,882	8,445	6	8	13	27	4,479
1914	549	7,686	8,235	3	9	27	39	6,388
1920	826	11,844	12,660	6	10	43	59	
1924	597	8,358	8,955	4	5	26	35	6,347
1929	1,403	19,642	21,045	10	18	44	66	7,319
1934	743	10,430	11,173	4	9	52	65	8,408
1939	790	11,000	11,790	6	9	48	63	9,334

Source: Harrison A.S.B. & Hunnard R.P.S., (1945) Valletta and Three Cities, A Report to accompany the outline plan for Valetta and the Three Cities region. Valletta: Government of Malta.

Figure 16. Some Evidence of Activity in Malta from 1879 to 1939.

Malta's Initial Defences

In the early 1930s, Malta was a major Royal Navy base. The belligerence of Italy towards Britain culminated with the meeting of Hitler and Mussolini in Venice on 14 June 1934. It was decided to strengthen the island's defences by providing Radar equipment, Anti-Aircraft, Coastal Defence, and Fighter Defence.

Before and during the Second World War, Malta developed a sophisticated defence system that helped the Allied Forces defeat Fascism and Nazism. Land, sea, and air forces coordinated with the civil authorities to create a defensive barrier that proved an impregnable fortress in stone.

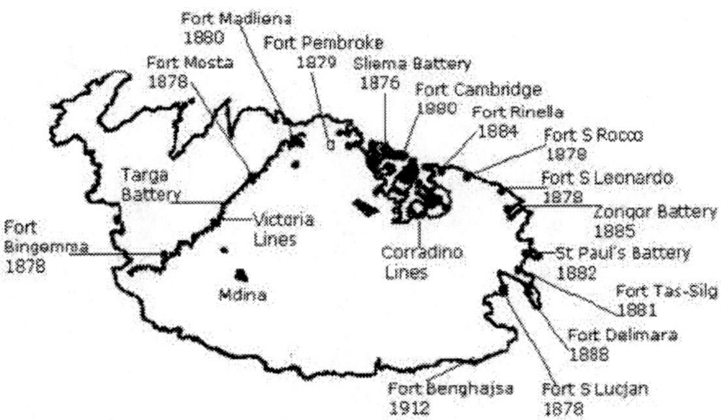

Source: 19th Century Fortifications (n.d.) *Maltese history and heritage* [ONLINE] Available at: https://vassallohistory.wordpress.com/fortifications/ [Accessed 01 January 2022].

Figure 17. Harbour Defences.

The Radar

The development of the radar contributed significantly to the Axis defeat. The British experimented with a radar prototype months before World War II broke out. These were the first radars to be tested outside the UK. As the War broke out, four more radars were brought into Malta to cover the high and low-level flying aircraft and the sea crafts.

In 1934 a 200-foot Mirror, known as 'Il Widna' (the Ear), was constructed. The first sound mirror is in Maghtab, roughly a mile or so inland with hills behind. It faces out to sea at a bearing of 20 degrees, towards Sicily around 60 miles away.

Its' construction started in the autumn of 1934 and was completed the following summer of 1935. Later in 1936, came the construction of a powerful telescope for enemy identification purposes. In March 1939, the first Air Ministry Experimental Station - Type MB1 - AMES No. 242 (or height angle aircraft searching) was mounted at Dingli Cliffs. In July 1939, the AMES 241 transportable Radar was installed. By mid-July 1941, the number of stations had increased by three: No. 501 AMES at Tas-Silġ, No. 502 AMES at Madliena and No. 504 AMES at Dingli, too (since Dingli is one of the highest points in Malta). The early RDF stations were Type GL. Mk. I and Mk. II. More radars were added as the Second World War progressed. Radar was then known as Radio Direction Finding (RDF) (Galea, 2002).

Source: Times of Malta (2017) *Key positions: Malta's World War II radars.* [ONLINE] Available at:https://timesofmalta.com/articles/view/key-positions-maltas-world-war-ii-radars.651667 [Accessed 01 January 2022].

Figure 18. Tas-Silg no 21033 AMES. Type 13.

Source: Times of Malta (2017) *Key positions: Malta's World War II radars.* Available at:https://timesofmalta.com/articles/view/key-positions-maltas-world-war-ii-radars.651667.

Figure 19. Il-Widna.

Source: Reemt Peters-Hein, R. (year unknown). *Radar Station at Dingli Cliffs.* Available at: https://www.locationscout.net/malta/4723-radar-station-at-the-dingli-cliffs.

Figure 20. Radar Station at Dingli Cliffs.

Anti-Aircraft and Coastal Defences

By June 1940, there were 34 Heavy Anti Aircraft guns and 8 Bofors, and several searchlights. Coastal defence guns were deployed at the following forts:

Benghisa
St. Leonardo
Madliena
Bingemma
Delimara
Ricasoli
Tigne
Campbell
St. Rocco
St. Elmo

Source: Abela A., (1942) 3LAA Regiment, Royal Malta Artillery.

Figure 21. The Royal Malta Artillery Upper Barakka, 1942.

Fighter Defence and Airfields

On April 19 1940, a Fighter Flight was officially established with its first 4 Gladiator biplanes. Two more were added in mid-June 1940. The following Airfields were present on the island:

Hal-Far
Ta' Qali
Luqa
Marsa Race Course (used for emergency landing)
Safi
Qrendi
Xewkija (Gozo). (This was a temporary airstrip construction in 1943[1])

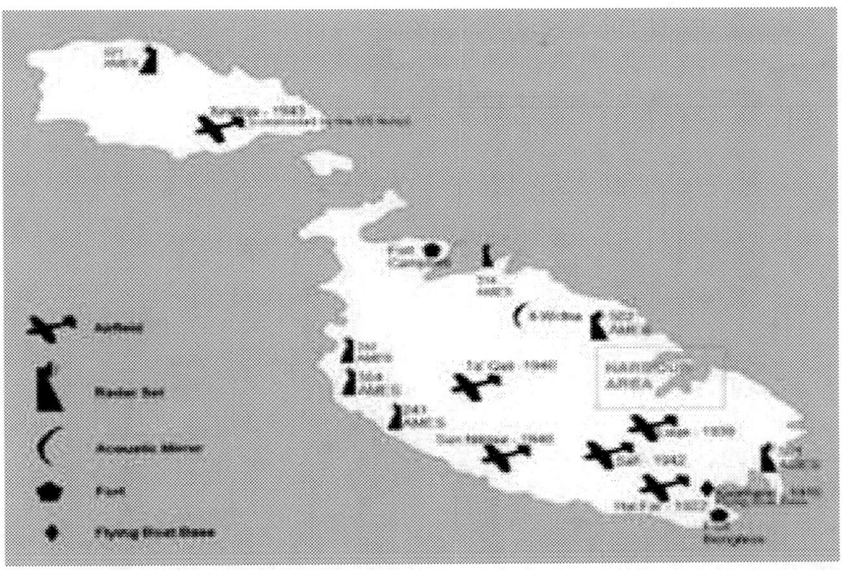

Source: 19th Century Fortifications (date unknown) *Maltese history and heritage* [ONLINE].
Available at: https://vassallohistory.wordpress.com/fortifications/
[Accessed 01 January 2022].

Figure 22. Defences outside the Harbour Area.

---

[1] *After the Battle,* Issue No. 10, 1975.

As the war progressed, the importance of Malta grew substantially. The Island was the base from which a concerted assault by RAF and Fleet Air Arm aircraft and Royal Navy submarines was launched against the Axis supply lines across the Mediterranean from Italy to North Africa. These attacks played an important part in hampering Rommel's forces in North Africa and greatly assisted General Montgomery in his final drive for victory, which began at El Alamein in October 1942. From Malta, reconnaissance sorties were flown, which led to the destruction of the Italian Fleet at Taranto by the Fleet Air Arm. In 1943, Malta was the launching pad for the invasion of Sicily nicknamed 'Operation Husky' (Zarb Dimech, 2008).

On 26 January 1940, Air Commodore F. H. M. Maynard, AFC, a New Zealand officer in the Royal Air Force, was appointed to Malta as Air Officer Commanding, Royal Air Force, Mediterranean. Maynardhad served in the air force for a long time. He had joined the Royal Naval Air Service in 1915, and had served two tours of duty in the Middle East during the inter-war years and held various commands in the United Kingdom Air Defence. He came to Malta from the Air Ministry (Zarb Dimech, 2008).[2]

Source: Louis Cordina Melitensia Collector (the original source of the photo is unknown).

Figure 23. Kalafrana Seaplane Slipway, Birzebbuga.

---

[2] *Victoria University of Wellington website* (The official history of New Zealand during the Second World War).

Chapter 4

Maltese Construction Work at RAF Stations in Malta during WWII

The Malta Independent published the article 'Maltese Construction Work at RAF Stations in Malta During WWII' in June 2008, citing material from a private collection of RAF Contracts, Mr Simon Cusens and the Victoria University of Wellington website. The piece is a tribute to Malta, which served as a staging area for a coordinated invasion in 1942. This chapter contains excerpts from this article.

The Contracts

Malta presented unique challenges for an Air Commander. It appeared to be a small and simple target from the air, measuring about seventeen miles by nine miles and covering around 95 square miles. Comino and Gozo two islands off the north-western edge of Malta, were ideal for orienting an arriving pilot. The four military objectives, including the Grand Harbour and three airfields, were restricted to the eastern part of this narrow territory, connected only by dusty and winding roads. The airfields were in bad condition. Hal Far was a short strip of land on the south shore, bounded by rocky outcrops and ravines. Ta' Qali, to the north, was built on a site surrounded on three sides by hills and familiar to Italian civil pilots. It had been built on the site of an old lake, and its grassy surface was marshy. Despite the bleak outlook, Air Commodore Maynard constructed a bomber airstrip at Luqa, in the island's central region, overlooking Valletta and the Grand Harbour.

Because the entire region had to be levelled from hills and quarries, this was a feat of resourcefulness. The airfield was surrounded by villages, each with its enormous church. There were no tools to build the airfield, but the most primitive Maltese working methods with horse and cart - the horse and carriage (il-karrozzin) seemed to be one thing, but the mule and cart were a more common meansof transport during World War II. They succeeded in building the longest runway on the island, with 1200 yards of tarmac. Aircraft dispersion was a serious issue due to the island's poor terrain and weak soil which was needed for food crops. Malta's stonewalled roads, on the other hand, were put to good use in establishing the famous Hal Safi strip, which connected Luqa and Hal Far airfields in a one-of-a-kind dispersal area. In addition, the fleet was camouflaged on the ground by the many mature Carob trees along the sides.

Chev. Angelo Grima was charged with its constructionand other Maltese companies, such as Galea Brothers on Sliema's Blanche Street, imported bathroom furnishings and fittings, lavatories, sinks, closets, bathtubs, and other items and served as government and military contractors. They also sold contemporary fireplaces, concrete pipes, bannisters, and wall tiling to wholesale and retail customers. One invoice in May 1940 pertains to products sold to Messrs. Anthony Falzon and Joseph Grima, Chev. Angelo Grima's brother. These items were utilized in the contractor's work on the tenders he was granted (Zarb Dimech, 2008).

Source: Ellis F.L. (n.d.). *Il-karrozzin* [ONLINE] Available at: https://www.guidememalta.com/en/13-pre-1950s-photos-of-malta-showing-what-life-was-like-back-then [Accessed 01 January 2022].

Figure 24. Mule and Cart, 1933.

After the war, the Wing Commander Superintending Engineer advised the contractor in a letter dated 28/2/1944 that the horses and carts provided under these contracts were to cease in February 1944, as per the contracts signed in 1943. Because they were the launching pad for the Allied air force, the RAF stations were the focus of concerted attacks by the Axis powers. The airfields' night and day air strikes in the second and third weeks of March 1942 were brutal. Airfields resembled lunar landscapes, and the civilian population suffered from carpet-bombing (Zarb Dimech, 2008).

Due to the air strikes, Maltese contractors could not complete their job by the agreed-upon time. Chev. Angelo Grima, the contractor, demanded reimbursement for the wasted time. One of the restrictions the contractor had to meet was that by 9 a.m. the day after any air attack, he had to provide a report detailing all the working hours lost, when production halted, the identities of the workers on the site, and the salary rate. A specific contract was the one in 'Wied Dalam', for which the Air Ministry was compensated. However, the contractor claimed that his claims on a substantial proportion of his wartime contracts for additional costs was not fulfilled. He also indicated that the amount was significant and often made the difference between losing and recovering expenditures on several of his contracts.

The Air Ministry, Directorate of Works, and Air Headquarters Royal Air Force of Malta were all under the control of the Air Office Commanding Mediterranean for the Under Secretary of State for Air. This establishment was located at 2 Castille Place in Valletta and was in charge of various aerodromes and other air force facilities. Under the leadership and cooperation of the Royal Engineers, civil engineering work in these key military zones was contracted to Maltese workers and Maltese enterprises (Zarb Dimech, 2008).

Lascaris War Room, Kalafrana, Hal Far Air Field, Luqa Airfield, and Ta' Qali Airfield were among the most notable Air Force Stations on the island. The Air Ministry Works Office was located At 'Marlborough House' Ta' Xbiex[3]. The implications on Malta might not have been as disastrous if there had not been signs of Italy's participation in the war. Maltese contractors working on R.A.F Stations in Malta felt the brunt of the war conditions, working with scarce resources and selflessly continuing to carry out their work to honour their contracts, realizing the national interest involved and disregarding the financial aspect as of secondary importance.

---

[3] It is noted that in Gozo an airfield was built and this is the only airstrip to have ever existed on the island of Gozo, up to the time of writing of the book The Gozo Airfield, 2004 by Charles Bezzina. This airstrip was necessitated by Operation Husky, the codename of the plan for the invasion of Sicily and the occupation of Italy. It was built in June 1943 between Xewkija and Nadur by the American E. Company of the 21st Regiment of the Air Force Engineers (APO 528) and a large gang of local labourers. This was terminated in a record time on 20 June, when the two planned runways were ready to receive the first Spitfires.

Chapter 5

The Assaults on Malta

The Assaults on Malta (1940-1943)

Malta's role in Hitler's and Mussolini's dream of conquering Europe and the world must be seen in the context of Hitler's 'continental policy', the invasion of the Balkans and the capture of Crete, accompanied by the deployment of the German air force in Italy. The beginning of the first infiltration of the German Air Force into Italy took place as early as June 1940, and immediately, Malta fell prey to the attacks of the Italian Air force on June 11 of the same year. On entry of Italy into the war against France and Britain, a liaison staff, known as *Italuft*, was set up under the command of General von Pohl. However, it was not until October 1940 that the first German flying units appeared in Italy when a transport unit was moved to Foggia to assist in ferrying Italian troops and equipment to Albania. Looking at the German air force in the Mediterranean campaigns of 1941, the battle for air supremacy and the battle for Malta stand out.

The First Assault (January 1941 to February 1941)

From the files of the German Air Ministry, Historical Section (*8th Abteilung*), the main objectives to dispatch Fliegerkorps X to Sicily in January 1941 to aid the Italians were threefold:

- To neutralize Malta as a base for British air and naval forces and thus to secure the Axis supply from Italy to North Africa
- To interfere with the British Supply route to Egypt
- To support the Axis armies in North Africa[4]

---

[4] The Rise and Fall of the German Air Force (1933-1945), issued by the Air Ministry (A.C.A.S. [T]), 1948.

They were aimed primarily at the harbour and installations of Valletta and the airfield on Malta. These attacks continued from January to March 1941, but the attacks failed to paralyze the island's defences.

The Second Assault (January 1942 to April 1942)

The unsuccessful elimination of Malta was the key to the Germans not achieving their goals in the Mediterranean. Since April 1941, when the Germans withdrew from Sicily, British aircraft based in Malta had caused considerable damage to the loading and unloading ports for the supply of raw materials to Rommel's forces in North Africa by attacking the harbours and other military installations (e.g., at Naples and Tripoli). Moreover, reconnaissance aircraft had also been able to observe and follow the passage of Axis convoys to Africa, thus enabling considerable success by British air and naval forces in attacking this traffic.

The HMS Illustrious Blitz (1941)

Source: Armoured Aircraft Carriers in World War II (n.d.) *The damaged HMS Illustrious sits in a dock under a large crane as bombs burst in the city of Valletta about her.* [ONLINE] Available at: https://www.armouredcarriers.com/illustrious-blitz-january-12-21 [Accessed 01 January 2022].

Figure 25. Bombing on the Grand Harbour.

The Luftwaffe attacking force ranged against Malta, consisting of 190 long-range bombers and 30 Ju. 87 dive bombers had maintained an average daily effort of 130 sorties throughout April 1942, after opening with over 300 sorties on March 21. Despite the increase in intensity and ferocity of the attacks during April 1942, Malta operations were not without their effects on the German Air Force. Some 300-400 aircraft were kept actively and heavily engaged during the greater part of the period from January to May 1942.

The figure above shows the damaged HMS Illustrious Blitz (1941) sitting in a dock under a large crane as bombs burst in the city of Valletta around it. Shattered by more and heavier bomb hits than any other carrier, HMS Illustrious nevertheless managed to contain her fires, stem the flooding and limp into the relative safety of Malta.

> "The Illustrious, battle-scarred but triumphant made port today after fighting off waves of German dive bombers for seven hours in the Straits of Sicily. Goering's Luftwaffe had swooped out of the sky in this first Mediterranean action and had given her one of the severest poundings ever delivered from the air against a single ship." (Armoured Aircraft Carriers in World War II)[5]

The Dockworkers were told to ensure the carrier, which lay crippled alongside the Parlatorio Wharf, where the red china dock is today, is seaworthy enough to make it to a safer port of Alexandria. Firefighters tried to put out the still-burning fires, doctors and ambulance men attended to the wounded, stretcher-bearers and seamen from other ships carried them, surveyors to see to the first needs of this difficult task of making the ship seaworthy, and others who in one way or another had a job to do.

All worked their way through the forest of bent, torn and blackened steel. At daybreak that morning, the Maltese dockyard workers took over. Their specific orders were to take care of only the bare necessities in order to be able to leave the port quickly.

Senior Engineer Lt-Cdr Martin oversaw the repairs. Admiralty diver Mr Joseph, who was later related to the Grima family through his daughter who married Joseph Grima (Jnr), son of Angelo's brother Joseph Grima, was tasked to inspect the hull of the aircraft carrier to look for damages that may have been caused to the hull.

Mr Gauci, who was some 20 feet below the water surface, knew that if the Illustrious was bombed again while he was beneath her hull, even a near-miss would send a shockwave through the water that would kill him instantly. The heavy equipment he wore would have ruled out any escape. He declined

[5] *The damaged HMS Illustrious sits in a dock under a large crane as bombs burst in the city of Valletta about her.* Available at: https://www.armouredcarriers.com/illustrious-blitz-january-12-21.

suggestions to be brought up to the surface even though bombs were bursting through the water surface. After 90 minutes under the carrier, he returned to the surface bleeding from the nose and ears. Even then, he refused medical treatment and went straight to report the findings. Nonetheless, he completed the job before the next raid, and the dockyard workers were able to complete the work on patching-up the carrier. For this bravery, he was made O.B.E. in 1943 (Armoured Aircraft Carriers in World War II).

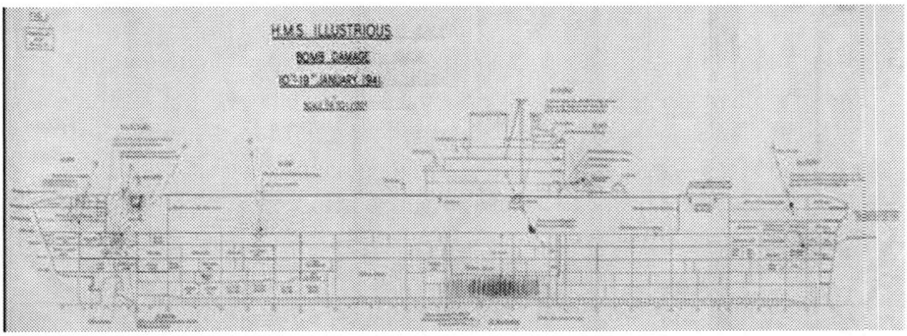

Source: Armoured Aircraft Carriers in World War II (n.d.) *DUBIOUS REFUGE Part 2: The Stuka bombing of HMS Illustrious* [ONLINE].
Available at: https://www.armouredcarriers.com/illustrious-blitz-january-12-21 [Accessed 01 January 2022].

Figure 26. Damages Sustained by the HMS Illustrious.

Source: Author's compilation.

Figure 27. Medal received by Mr Gauci.

Source: Gal, J. (1958) Večer. [ONLINE] Available at: https://www.vecer.com/ reference number 107939 [Accessed 01 January 2022].

Figure 28. Standard Diving Equipment dress Oswalt, Slovenia (1958).

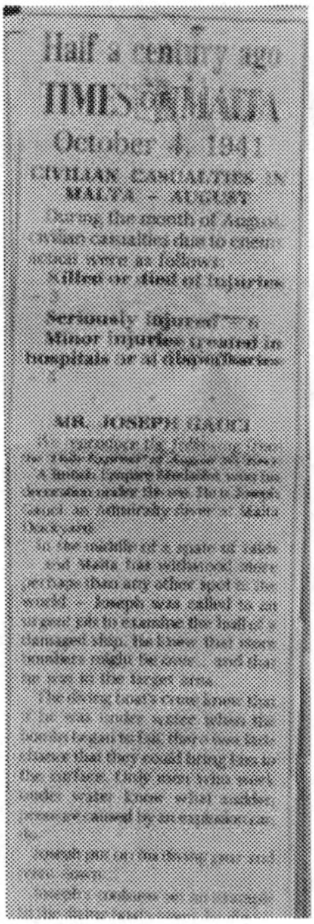

Half a century ago
TIMES OF MALTA
October 4, 1941

CIVILIAN CASUALTIES IN MALTA - AUGUST

During the month of August civilian casualties due to enemy action were as follows:

Killed or died of injuries

Seriously injured

Minor injuries treated in hospitals or at dispensaries

MR. JOSEPH GAUCI

[illegible]

Source: Times of Malta, (1941) Archives.

Figure 29. Extract from the Times of Malta.

Source: Author's Compilation.

Figure 30. Joseph Gauci (Admiralty diver).

The Malta Convoy of 1942 and the Final Assault

Perhaps the best impression that one can obtain of Malta's importance in the whole Mediterranean and North African campaign is by studying the island's being 'a thorn in the enemy's side' by preventing war supplies from reaching North Africa. In turn, the Axis forces did their utmost to prevent convoys from reaching Malta. The convoys supplying Malta kept the offensive against Axis supply convoys passing from Italy and Sicily to North Africa.

During the first four months of 1942, if a British supply vessel did succeed in reaching Malta safely, the subsequent unloading operations were subjected to continued bombing and were rendered extremely difficult.

The island had to wait until the middle of June - when air attack had abated - for the next attempt to supply it on a large scale. In June, the operation to supply Malta was a double one: a convoy of six merchant ships passing from the United Kingdom through the Straits of Gibraltar and another of 11 merchant ships from Egypt were to reach Malta on consecutive days. Enemy attention would thus be divided between the two convoys. In the end, only two ships arrived.

The final supply convoy to be sent to Malta under these conditions was in August 1942 and consisted of 14 merchant ships with an escort of 3 aircraft carriers with 72 fighter aircraft together with 2 battleships, 6 cruisers, an anti-aircraft ship and 24 destroyers. From the air point of view, with a force of some 700 aircraft available to the Germans and Italians, the passage of this convoy bid fair to be a major action. Between August 13 and 15, the convoy reached Malta. The five remaining supply vessels from the original fourteen were unloaded, but the enemy made no serious attempt to interfere; the British fighter strength in Malta was such as to discourage direct attacks on the island.

a

b

Source: The Malta Independent. (2017) *Santa Marija Convoy: 75th anniversary, one of Malta's most seminal WWII moment approaches.* [ONLINE] Available at: https://www.independent.com.mt/articles/2017-07-30/local-news/Santa-Marija-Convoy-75th-anniversary-one-of-Malta-s-most-seminal-WWII-moment-approaches-6736177204 [Accessed 01 January 2022].

Figure 31a, 31b. Santa Maria Convoy.

In a letter dated April 13, 2003, in the Sunday Times of Malta under the signature of Mr B.T. Gibbs, praising the skills of Maltese civilian workers who helped defend the islands, epitomizes and immortalizes on black and white the Maltese workers' skills and bravery under war conditions. Mr Gibbs goes into quite some detail in explaining the contribution made by the Maltese workers to the Royal Army Ordinance Corps (ROAC). The skilled and semi-skilled Maltese personnel were based at MIRA building (then Mamo's) at Gzira and a site adjacent to the Army Barracks at St. Andrew's and included tradesmen such as carpenters, blacksmiths, tinsmiths, fitters, welders, radio and electrical repairers and others.

In the genuine spirit of the George Cross Island, Mr Patrick Gibbs concludes his letter with a compliment to civilian craftsmen who made a vital contribution to Malta's defence when they and their families were facing hardship and were exposed to danger (Holland, 2003).

Chapter 6

The Maltese Construction Trade

The extent of megalithic architecture in Malta, such as Hagar Qim and Mnajdra, is sufficient proof that construction was always an important industry in Malta. The Ggantija temples in Gozo are the oldest freestanding structures in the world, predating Stonehenge in Britain and the Great Pyramids in Egypt by hundreds of years.On 8 February 1941, Prime Minister Churchill of Britain wrote a message to President Roosevelt of the United States where he coined up the now-famous phrase, ‘Give us the tools, and we will finish the job’. The scarcity of war implements was also felt in Malta as much as in Britain since the day Italy declared war on the Allies.

Tools, Skills and Resources

Mr Salvatore Spiteri of the Mason’s Class appears to have used a tiny copybook with notes in Maltese regarding the abilities necessary in construction work as a very useful teaching tool. He preserved handwritten notes from the 1940s regarding the use of Maltese masonry know-how and practices. This copybook served as an excellent beginning point for learning about the individuals’ abilities. Most of the work dealt with in this copybook was common to most books on elementary science. The close association with building tools and the treatment of many simple building problems was an important part of the teaching to economise on time, improve the instruction and retain the student’s interest throughout. Also, the association with building terms, especially those used in the Maltese construction trade and materials used was obvious and in such a form as to appeal to the young student whose acquaintance with the actual building practice was not so extensive.[6]

The exigencies of our post-modern economy have put aside much of the work described in this book to make way for modem projects. One such

---

[6] Experimental Building Science, by J. Leask Manson, Volume One, Introduction to Science as applied in building, Cambridge at the University Press, 1945. This volume was found sufficient for the first two years’ work in Building Science in National Certificate Courses in Britain.

instance is the total disappearance from the map of the Kalafrana seaplane base that has made way for the Freeport. Other sites have been victims of neglect, pillaging and vandalism and requests for re-development. The Malta Environment and Planning Authority has afforded protection to a number of properties of a historical military nature, such as the Officer's Mess at Fort Campbell, Mellieha, St. George's Barracks, St. Julian's and the Underground Flourmill, St. Paul's, to mention a few.[7]

Even though modern technology has gradually displaced the skills of the stonemason, this does not mean that these skills are no longer needed. A very interesting feature in the Sunday Circle of November 2009 gives a succinct overview of Gozitan master stonemason Leli Saliba (known as il-Bufajra), who has been restoring crumbling stone structures for several years, bringing them back to life. This Feature also lists restoration works to protect Malta's heritage and environment sponsored by different organizations.[8] The Limestone Heritage is also a very good example of the history of limestone in Malta.[9]

A list of some of the tools used gives an idea of what was required at hand[10]:

Fies (Mason's pickaxe or mattock with one end thin-pointed and a two-inch-wide cutting edge at the other)

Marlocc tal-fies (the wooden handle of the pickaxe)

Invel(Spirit-level)

Baqqun (Pickaxe)

Rebekkin (Manual driller)

Kaxxi tal-Kejl (Boxes used in measuring)

Slielen (Ladders)

Imasqa (Soil digger)

żappun (Mattock with a jutting edge used for breaking up clotted dust). Masons use it for mixing plaster.

---

[7] Planning Authority Malta.

[8] Sunday Circle issued with the Sunday Times of Malta, November 2009. The Article mentions the Alfred Mizzi Foundation, Din l-Art Helwa, Qala Local Coundl and the MEPA Environmental Fund as some of the organizations helping in the protection of Malta's heritage and environment.

[9] Limestone Heritage is the first systematic attempt to document the history of use of the building limestone of Malta. It is situated in a disused soft stone quarry in Siggiewi, part reclaimed back for agrarian use, a rehabilitation technique used in local quarries since time immemorial.

[10] Translations into the Maltese of the technical terms used in the Maltese building trade were taken from Maltese-English Dictionary, by Joseph Aquilina, MidSea Books Ltd., 1987.

Rigi/Rutelli (Measuring tapes/rulers)
Skwerra (Masons L-Shaped or T-shaped measuring rod (metal or wood). It is a tool for measuring angles.
Pali Zghar (Small spades)
Landi tal-Petrol (Petrol jerrycans)
Karrijiet (Carts)
Imtieraq (Stone-cutter's hatchet generally handled with both hands usually having a short handle)
Imqassijiet (Scissors)
Mazza (Hammer)
Cappa (Iron support)
Spnar (Tapered large nail with edges varying in size from 3 to 10 inches used in rock cutting)
Lexxun/lexxuna (Weeding hoe used to clear up soil and small stone)

The Maltese worker had to learn the skills required for construction in three ways: civil, naval, and military. In this sense, construction was taught in its most basic form, i.e., how to build bridges and other works of wood, wrought iron and stone, which included the building of churches, theatres and houses. Limestone is the most important industrial mineral in the Maltese archipelago. There are two types: hard stone and soft stone. Both are calcareous and of uniform colour. Since time immemorial, they have been used as a building material, particularly as dimension stones. Given the absence of other building materials, such as wood etc., limestone has been used to build walls and elevation building elements and as a roofing material. Its beauty and workability have long been known. There is even a tradition of exporting it to other countries for use as building stone.

Styles of Ornament and Structures

The time which had elapsed since the end of the First World War and the beginning of the Second World War saw a great expansion on the subject of Building Science, as technical instruction for scientific research and in practical applications for architecture and building. Much instruction introduced in an elementary form had been developed almost beyond recognition, and at the start of the Second World War, there was a wealth of advanced technical knowledge and experimental material not previously available. The construction of docks, forts, bridges, and breakwaters is also considered part of civil engineering. The copybook starts by giving an outline of the different styles of ornament used in building, notably Greek and Roman. The Greeks conquered the world with their art, the Romans with politics and their legions. Until the present day, the whole civilised world is striving to emulate the works of art of the former. The latter's laws are considered throughout the world as the foundation upon which all laws must be established.

In these facts lies the difference in the character of the two peoples. The Romans who lived at the beginning of Roman history, could not develop an independent art for all their efforts were directed towards accumulating wealth and enlarging their lands. Therefore, they were obliged to take the motifs for their art from Etruria and continued to do so until Grecian art became predominant.

Becoming more accustomed to luxury from the conquests they made, the Romans gradually began to form a national art of their own under the guidance of Greek teachers. The practical spirit of the Romans and their taste for monumental work are seen best exemplified in their architecture, a science in which they have performed the most magnificent work, especially in connection with the monumental development of temples, basilicas, *thermae*, theatre etc. The Romans adopted the three columnar Orders of the Greeks, retaining, however, the Etruscan column.[11] To these four orders, they added the Composite order. The five orders are:

Tuscan
Doric
Ionian
Corinthian
Composite

Each of these styles has three different aspects: the Column, Pedestal, and the Entablature. For each of these three, there are other subdivisions. The Pedestal or *Stilobat* serves to keep the column up to a certain height above ground level and is made of three parts: *Kuruna* (a wide strip on the underside of a moulding), *Dadu* (cube of a pedestal between base and cornice) and the *Baziment* (foundation or base of a column between shaft and pedestal). The column is the main part and is also made of three parts: *Kaptel* (head or cornice of pillar or column), *Xaft* (shaft), *Bazi* (base). The base supports the column,

[11] The Styles of Ornament by Alexander R. Speitz (ed. R. Phene Spiers), 1910.

and the *Kaptel* serves to support the upper part of the structure, which is the *Entablature*. The *Entablature* comprises the *Gwarinicun* (ornamental outline in cornices of building or projecting moulding continued horizontally along the face of a building marking the termination of the top storey), *Friz, Arkitraf.* The *Arkitraf* is composed of stones that reach out from one column to another. The *Gwarincun* protrudes more than the other two and serves as a shelter against the rain both to itself and the other structure parts.

Measurements

The most convenient way to measure the different parts of the structure is through the *Modulu*. The length of the *Modulu* is equal to half the diameter, i.e., the Race of the lower section of the column.

Many designs of the five main Orders of Classical Architecture were put up by architect Giacomo Barozzi of Vignola (known as Vignola), and his spectacular drawings were utilized as models for this type of work. Giacomo Barozzi was born in Vignola, Emilia-Romagna, near Modena. He began his architectural career in Bologna by painting and creating perspective templates for inlay artists to support himself. In 1536, he went to Rome for the first time to create measured drawings of Roman temples to publish an illustrated Vitruvius. He gave the following heights for each Order so that each small part of the structure is measured accurately:

Tuscan	14 Modules
Doric	16 Modules
Ionic	18 Modules
Corinthian	2 Modules
Composite	20 Modules

The five orders, engraving from Vignola's Regola delle cinque ordini d'architettura (Vernd, 2003).

Other subjects covered in this copybook include the construction of *Pilastri* (pillar, pier, post-column or any load-bearing vertical mass of masonry isolated from the wall. Doors and their positioning in the facade (design aspects depending on the use, position, shape, proportion and decoration).

Source: Saxon State and University Library (1924) German Photo Library. [ONLINE] Available at: www.deutschefotothek.de [Accessed 01 January 2022].

Figure 32. The five orders, Vignola 1640

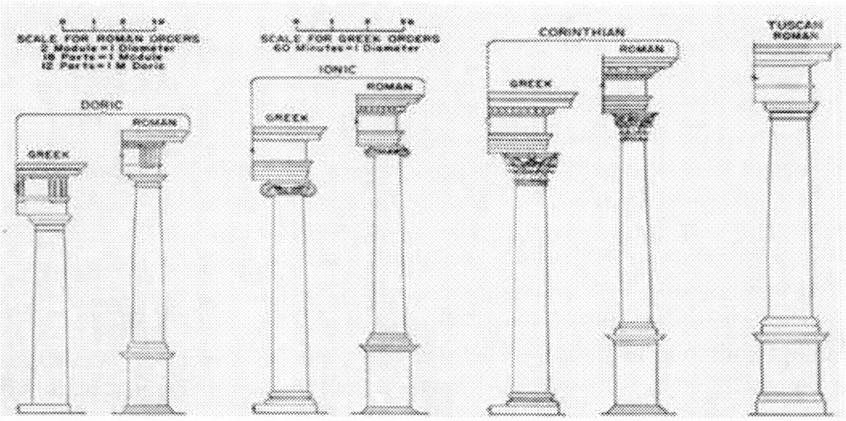

Source: The Orders of Classical Architecture. (Original photo source unknown) [ONLINE] Available at: http://designerlea.blogspot.com/p/proportion-scale.html [Accessed 01 January 2022].

Figure 33. The Orders.

Walls

Important emphasis was placed on the building techniques using the small *kantun* of 9 inches and the *kantun doblu* of 1 foot.

Terms used in this trade were:

- *Hitan tal vażi* (Walls built using stones larger than the smaller slabs or *kantun.* It is also the base of an arch or box of a column)
- Gebel *mahdum skorra* (angled structures)
- *Is-Soll ta' tieqa* (window sill).

The use of the *Hitan Doblu* (a thick wall having two skins or double the usual thickness) was to strengthen the outer structure of the building and prevent humidity from entering.

Saff tal-Qatran (layer of tar humidity to prevent from rising from beneath the building)

Roofs and Ceilings

These were divided into three categories:

- *Hnejjiet* (Arches) are used mostly in large water reservoirs and sometimes in large underground storages, and they were designed to support huge weights
- *Travi ta' l-Injam* (Wooden beams) Information about the laying of beams and their treatment by tar
- *Travi tal-hadid* (Iron beams).

Limestone Used in Paving

- *Gebel tal-Franka*, (Limestone used in the *Canġatura,* which is 1 foot 9 inches square.)
- *Gebel tal-Qawwi* (coralline limestone such as the *żonqor tal-prima*, very hard and compact limestone of crystalline texture, sometimes of flinty texture with conchoids fracture, impermeable or almost impermeable to water, constituting the lower layer of Malta's lower coralline limestone and the middle and upper sub-layers of the upper coralline and from which an excellent hard stone, very useful for paving footpaths, for breaking up into macadam as road-metal, and for the construction of docks as well as for other works requiring great

resistance to weight or to the action of the weather or sea. The *żonqor tas-sekonda,* a type of limestone often crystalline, but more commonly sacchariod, constituting the upper and softer layer of Malta's lower coralline limestone and the middle and upper layers of the upper coralline and very much used for the production of lime.)

Madum Tas-Siment (Cement Tiles)

When the pavement was laid and ready, it was washed by the *halib tat-tajn* (a milky mixture of water and clay) in order to fill in the *fili* (space between one block of stone and another in a wall) and after it was *invjat* (polished and levelled off) well and a sponge wet with linseed oil was used to give two coatings to protect the finish. When the hard and compact limestone (*ġebel tal-qawwi*) was used, linseed oil was applied.

Stairways

- Stairway held by two *irjus* (the heads of quadrangular building stones).
- Stairway held by one *ras*.
- *Taraġ* round (*garigor* or second stairway)

Raw Materials

Apart from the tools, the following resources were required to complete the works. This list is based on wartime (1940-1943) data.

Kerosene

Kerosene was used for driving various machinery, i.e., winches, compressors, tractors etc. and was consumed at the rate of 100 gallons per week. According to the official documents, the purchase was 50 gallons, and anything above that had to be purchased through other sources at £15 per 40 gallons.

Edible Oil

Edible oil was used for lighting purposes in the underground workings as it would give off no fumes injurious to the workers. On August 1st 1940, the price was increased from 1/Sd. to 30/- per gallon.

Timber

The price of timber for shuttering rose from 7d. to 2/- per foot super.

Spalls and Sand for Concrete

This material was used on underground chambers. The price rocketed, and the contractor hired a small crusher and produced spalls on site. This constituted a saving for the contractor, especially regarding delivery charges.

Soft Limestone ('Franka')

This was the most important resource for masonry. Up to the 8th November 1940, the price was 4¼d per ft. cube. This was increased to S½d. and subsequently to 9d. on the 1st of March 1941. When exposed to the elements, the soft limestone is eaten away over time and has to be removed or changed as it is less capable of resisting storm, sea, and salt as the harder *tal-qawwi.*

Lime and Sand

Slaked lime for use in masonry could be purchased for 2/- per salm (16 cube. Ft.). In August 1940 this price was increased to 25/- per salm. The sand was used for mortar in masonry and plastering. Before the war broke out in 1940, sand was also imported from Sicily.

Shingle

Shingle was used to construct the English style roofing, and the entire surface area in cubic yards had to be known before an order was placed. During 1935 quantities of Messina shingle were ordered from Sicily by the contractor on request by the Royal Engineers Office. Order of the 11th of July 1935 was for 179 cu.yds. of Messina Shingle for delivery near Pembroke Old Fort and to Road behind the N.A.A.F.I. Order of the 19th of July 1935 was made for 30 cu. yds of Messina Shingle to Hal-Far R.A.F. Station.

Order during August 1935 for 35 cubic yards at Calafrana.

During the unloading of a shingle in December 1936, a heap of the material was deposited at Ras Hanżir, Marsa, because when the contractor with his lorries loaded with shingle, men were lowering the wire netting through the sea, the traffic was suspended for nearly the whole week, and the contractor could not deliver any shingle. The contractor gave this information to the Royal Engineer to explain the delay in delivering the shingles for this order.

Another order as for the supply of 34 cubic yards of Messina shingle at Tas Sile.

Gunpowder and Safety Fuse

The acquisition of sufficient gunpowder and safety fuse for the work constituted one of the chief problems for the contractor. After the entry of Malta into the active war zone (11 June 1940), it became impossible for the contractor to obtain gunpowder from normal sources due to the extreme shortage on the Island. Consequently, the contractor was obliged to purchase both gunpowder and safety fuse.

This was chiefly manufactured locally, and its quality was in no way effective as English manufactured gunpowder. Locally manufactured gunpowder was normally composed of several ingredients, mainly carbon usually obtained from local grapevines. In addition to this, the powder was in such demand that it was not given sufficient time to be properly dried. Gelignite and prime cord were unobtainable, and electricity was unavailable for detonation.

Petrol and Oil

During his work, the contractor used 100 gallons of petrol weekly, purchased from the Shell Company until the 8th November 1941. From 9th November 1941 until 25th March 1943, the contractor withdrew petrol upon repayment from R.A.F sources. However, the amount of petrol allowed to him was only half the amount needed to keep transport operating, and to the period ending 31st March 1943, he had to buy petrol through whatever source could be found at 5/6 per gallon. Petrol was essential to keep all transport moving, as the chief feature of the underground work was the speed at which excavated material could be removed so that blasting could be continuous.

Lubricating oil was purchased by the contractor from the Shell Company at the rate of 40 gals weekly until March 31st 1942. The oil was used for lubricating purposes and for mixing with kerosene as fuel oil. Diesel oil at this period was of such poor quality that it was of no use at all for the contractor's plant. The price of oil rose from 5/-per gal. on 31st July 1940 to 7/2 per gallon on January 1st 1942.

The Contractor

The contractors were either an individual firm or a company and included the executors and administrators of the individual or the members composing the firm as well as the assignees of the individual, firm or company. The definition of Admiralty meant the Commissioners for executing the Office of Lord High

Admiral of the United Kingdom of Great Britain and Ireland. The Superintending Officer was the person superintending the execution of the works on behalf of the Admiralty appointed by the Civil Engineer-in-Chief.

The practice was for the Secretary of State War Department through the Royal Engineers Office to invite contractors to tender for contracts.

By a letter dated 5th July 1937, the Major Royal Engineers, Deputy Commander, Reconstruction, informed contractors that the War Department was anxious to increase the number of Contractors for works service on the list for services exceeding Sterling 5,000 in value. He also asked the contractors if they would be interested for inclusion in this higher list, and if so, they were to furnish his office with a banker's reference. During April 1940, the Royal Engineer's Office, through the Surveyor of Works, asked contractors to enter into the contract by limited competition for the erection of Battery Barracks at San Pietru and San Giacomo.

Suppliers

The contractor depended heavily for the completion of works assigned to him on obtaining the material required for the job on the supply of the following materials and equipment and their servicing:

Lorries

Boulton & Paul Ltd.

Servicing of Vehicles

British Motor Company - Gzira
Joe Scicluna – Mosta

Gun Powder

Joseph Dalli, nickname, *iz-zoccrin* (Fireworks Manufacturer) – Gudja

Tiles

Michaelangelo Galea

Sand, Gravel and Lime

Salvatore Galea (Crotion Contractor) - Naxxar

Giuseppe Axisa (Army, Navy and Civil Contractor -Tarxien)

The contractor was also asked to import sand from Sicily up to the period before the start of the Second World War. One particular instance is the request made by Degiorgio & Azzopardi (Shell Installation -Birzebbugia).

Petrol

John Bull Ironmongery Stores

Clothing

Sartoria Francesco Milazzo & Figli –Valletta

Source: Vanderveen, B. (1930) Historic Military Vehicles Directory, Poland: After the Battle Publication.

Figure 34. Van Morris Commercial R- Type (Circa 1931) used by G.B. Pantalleresco during wartime Malta.

The Workforce

The hardships endured by the workers before and during wartime Malta brought about much consciousness of rights and better work conditions. This led to the development of trade unionism and, subsequently, a solid welfare state over the years. During 1943, trade unionism in Malta was born and firmly established by the setting up of the General Workers Union. Other unions at the time were the Dockyard and Imperial Workers Union and the Government Workers Union.

During August 1943, a strike was held, the main issue being that wages were not covering the cost of food rationing. The strike was eventually called off in order not to disrupt the war effort.

Transportation

Transportation and the means of transport were of utmost importance to keep up the pace of the work in progress both during peacetime and especially in wartime.

Animals were a means of saving on the scarce petrol supplies and made up for the lack of available lorries. An examination of a very detailed contract where the contractor offered to supply horses, mules carts and drivers to H.M. Dockyard, R.N Hospital, R.N. Armament Depot and other Naval Establishments in Malta for the period 27th November 1934 to 26th November 1935 gives a very good picture of the conditions of transportation by horses and mules.

Most of the journeys done under most of the contracts under this period were from Dockyard to the following points (Zarb Dimech, 2011):

Calafrana
Marsa
Ghajn Tuffieha
Ghargur Signal Station
Dingli Signal Station
Ricasoli Rifle Range
'Ta Sile' Signal Station
Manoel Island
Msida Torpedo Depot
Castille Signal Station

Verdala Barracks
Royal Navy Hospital
Casal Luca Reservoir

The Contractor's Men

The contractor was held responsible for the acts of his workmen and for all damage resulting from the execution of the contract to any buildings, embankments, bridges, railways, roads, fences, oil, water or gas mains or to any government or other property whatsoever and was to make good for all such damage in a perfect and professional manner at his own cost. The workmen were to obey the Dockyard Police (or Naval Police).

The men employed by the contactor were to be decently clad and approved by the Superintending Officer. The contractor was held responsible for their diligence, honesty, and good conduct. Drivers were to load and unload the carts. A properly qualified and English-speaking Agent empowered to act for the contractor was to be constantly employed. Orders and instructions given to the Agent were binding as if given to the contractor. No person less than twenty years of age was to be employed under this contract.

All tools were to be supplied by the contractor for the loading and unloading of materials, and these were to be marked in a distinctive manner that was to be approved by the Superintending Officers.

Horses, Mules and Carts

The contractor had to provide horses or mules, harnesses, carts and drivers, and extra labourers in the quantities required by the Superintending Officer. The horses or mules had to be robust, full-sized, well-made, not old or battered, but sound, well fleshed, in good shape, free of sores, and otherwise suited for the job. Horses were to be well-shod and fed and watered regularly by and at the Contractor's expense, but no time was to be spent shoeing, feeding, cleaning, harnessing, or watering the horses or mules during the Establishment's working hours unless an unavoidable accident or necessity occurred. At dinnertime, which was a time allowed to the workmen and after working hours every day, this time was dedicated to examining the feet of the horses or mules, their shoes put in order, and all this was at the expense of the Contractor (Zarb Dimech, 2011).

Loads and Depositing Areas

The carts had to be sturdy and well-made, with two wheels and with the ability to accommodate all services. To the satisfaction of the Superintending Officer, they were to be equipped with sturdy mobile boxes that were tight and fitted with sliding back-boards and huge recognizable marks. The boxes used to remove rubbish and transport of materials were of a standard size (4 feet by 3 feet by 1 foot 6 inches), and the materials were heaped to a height of six inches at the centre, above the top of the box. The standard load specified was 20 cubic feet equal to between 12 and 15 cwts, not including moveable loads in bags if these were permitted. All cars were to be fitted with boxes. The minimum load for removing miscellaneous stores was 12 carts, and the maximum load for one horse or mule was 15 cwts. The Contractor was to deposit the material tipped and roughly cut to acceptable levels or as specified on the Admiralty tip at the Corradino. The trash was to be removed from the areas mentioned by the Superintending Officer at a rate of not less than 30 cubic yards per day for each order (Zarb Dimech, 2011).

Working Hours

The horses or mules, carts, and drivers were to be ready to work in every way at the start of the working hours of the Establishments to which the contract pertained, as well as at such other times as may be ordered in writing. The horses, mules, and drivers were to stop working each day during the regular workmen's supper break and at the end of the working day. However, if needed, horses, mules, and drivers were asked to work earlier and after normal working hours at special rates established in Schedules, whether in the designated Establishments or in the completion of any travels required by H.M. Service (Zarb Dimech, 2011).

Mileage and Lost Time

A minimum speed of 3 miles per hour had to be maintained for one contract. If any time was lost, the officer who employed the cart or carts was required to subtract it from the time paid for the task. When carts were instructed to start work or be released from employment outside of a three-mile radius of Sheer Bastion at the Dockyard, time for travel for each cart was provided at the rate of one hour for every three miles (the distance was measured in a direct line from Sheer Bastion). The contractors who were invited to tender for contracts were to satisfy themselves as to the nature of the existing roads and all matters that would influence their tenders. No claim for extra payments made due to any misunderstanding or incorrect information on any of these points was entertained (Zarb Dimech, 2011).

Purchase of Lorries

It became necessary for the contractor to purchase lorries for use on the work as the workload intensified. The contractor purchased 12 lorries, which were from one to seven years old, for work on one contract. These lorries would have cost £440 under normal conditions but owing to war conditions, the price paid was £2900. During the work, some of these vehicles became derelict, and upon the completion of the job, the value of the remainder was less than £100.

As the war was looming on the horizon, a copy of a letter dated 16th February 1937 was sent to Angelo Grima as one of the major contractors. This letter was sent by the Major, Royal Engineer Offices informing Mr Grima that during the next few years contracts may have to be placed in circumstances where Time will be the deciding factor and also that it might not always be possible to lend any war department-owned mechanical aids (e.g., concrete mixers, compressor plants etc.,) to the successful tenderer as had been the case sometimes in the past. Furthermore, he informed him that only those firms that are known to have such mechanical aids and able to make full use of them would be invited to tender.

Sometimes and inevitably, a breakdown in a vehicle would occur, and the contractor would claim damages for, and in order not to interrupt the flow of the transport, he would hire another vehicle as was the case when a 5-ton lorry's wheel had to be replaced and until the replacement was made another truck was hired for the period 20th February 1939 up to 3rd March 1939.

The contractor also gave a list of drivers of lorries under his charge and employed in the fulfilment of contracts awarded to him. An example of this is Elidio Zammit of Casal Curmi driving Lorry No. 5535, who was employed at H.M. Dockyard since June 1939 working with this lorry under the Admiralty contract for the supply of carts and lorries. Special permission from the Traffic Superintendent was given to attend to his daily services.

Under the Black Out Order of 1939, motor vehicles were authorised to be driven during the ordinary black-out hours provided the lighting restrictions laid down in Government Notice no. 605 dated 7 December 1939 were complied with.

Complaints

It was not unusual for H.M. Dockyard to complain about removing accumulations of rubbish, such as in the letter dated 12th March 1938. The clearance of Chips and Shavings backlog was causing inconvenience, and the contractor, Mr Grima, was requested to give the matter immediate attention, giving him a deadline for clearance and the resultant forfeiture of the 20 Sterling Deposit on the consignment. The contractor had his good reasons to complain, as in the case of a contract for soft stone. Mr Angelo Grima brought to the notice of the Air Ministry, in a letter dated December 24, 1938, that delays in soft stone deliveries were happening due to the lack of paper chits showing the measurement of the stones (in cubic feet) for each trip to the driver of the lorry transporting stones. If such chits were accessible regularly, the contractor indicated that he would have been able to determine if orders were completed or not and keep weekly settlements with the quarry-man and avoid trouble and delivery errors. His stance was that the only records available were unofficial quarry-men records.

Another issue was that the contractor's attention was directed to the deteriorated state and tiny size of a number of the boxes, which were in use on the carts at Luqa airport, by a letter dated February 15, 1939, from the Superintending Engineer, Air Ministry, asking for a solution of this (Zarb Dimech, 2011).

Another curious and quite unusual situation was a letter from the Civil Engineer-in-Chief's Department of H.M. Dockyard of 12th January 1940 where the contractor Mr Grima was asked to cease deliveries under the contract for soft stone blocks of the Dingli Order because the figures supplied to the contractor showed the total quantity supplied as against the quantity ordered was higher, and therefore no further stone was required.

By a letter dated November 12, 1940, the contractor was instructed to hasten soft stone block deliveries because deliveries had been very poor in the previous weeks, particularly for stone to be supplied inside the Dockyard area. He was warned that a lack of stone was causing significant delays in completing key defence works, and he was instructed to enhance the current delivery rate. The contractor was ordered to arrange for an urgent stone delivery to finish orders at Ghajn Duieli Gate and Garden Reach (Zarb Dimech, 2011).

Horses and Cart

Carts were bought in variable amounts up to 200 per day for one contract, primarily during the Blitz's deadliest days, with the carts being used to move the stone to fill craters and maintain runways clear. The local authorities compensated some of the horses and carts that were damaged. From June 1940 to November 1942, there were 1,437 raids that lasted a total of 89½ working days. To keep horses from panicking and charging towards planes, the R.A.F. ordered all horses (whether or not with carts laden) to be unharnessed and tied. After the 'all clear,' this entailed re-harnessing (Zarb Dimech, 2011).

Transport of Workmen

In pre-war days, workmen travelled from their villages to work and home again under their arrangement. However, with the arrival of air raids, they refused to come to work unless transport to and from their homes was provided. This was common to other contractors and departments at this period. The contractor hired two buses at £5 per day for this purpose. In addition, he used 3 of his lorries for 2 hours each daily to transport men to and from their homes in the scattered villages on the western side of the island.

Chapter 7

Construction Contracts

Introduction

Contracts in construction projects set forth the parties' obligations to each other and determine the risk as distributed between the parties in the project. Entering into any business or service requires a written agreement to provide certainty, logic and mechanisms to mitigate risks. Of the many clauses that are included in construction contracts, the main ones pertain to the scope of work, payment terms, project price, change orders, material specifications and timeframes.

The writers identify the major contractual agreements relevant to the period covered in this book, including the sites of work services delivered and contracts awarded before, during and after WWII. The goal is to give readers a sense of the type of labour needed at the time and how it was accomplished.

Contracts Awarded before the Second World War

09-729- H.M. Dockyard - Supply of fine and coarse sand.

24/3/31- H.M Dockyard - Supply of 10 Cubic yards of clay of approved quality at 4/11d per cubic yard.

03/3/737 - H.M Dockyard - Demolition of hard stone chimney stock about 113 feet high (nos. 4 &5) Docks in H.M Dockyard and for the removal from Admiralty premises of all demolished stonework, fire brick lining and foundation concrete.

04/5/38 - Air Ministry - Erection of receipts and issue Stores and engine store building including incidental works at R.A.F Station, Calafrana.

24/11/38 - Shell Company (Malta) Limited - Agreement for the installation and lease of a kerbside pump no. 41 (Mark IV), tank and fittings for the Shell Company (Malta) Limited upon the premises known as Central Bar, Church Square Zejtun and the rental of same to the contractor. The installation of the underground tank had a capacity of 500 gallons together with one complete set of fittings, including Globe and electrical installation and one dipstick. This pump was used exclusively for the storage and supply of Shell Motor Products, and the contractor was to promote the sale of Shell Motor Oil and Greases as far as possible.

December 1938 –- Air Ministry - Erection and completion of combined dining room and institute at R.A.F Station, Siggiewi (Tas-Salvatur).

12/1/39 - H.M. Dockyard - Supply of first quality soft stone (tal-franka).

May 1939 - Air Ministry - Excavation for M.T & Aviation Petrol Storage Tanks and Pump House, including the Pump House construction at R.A.F Station Luqa. In excavating trenches and running cables for telephone and electric light old soft stone slabs were used to cover buried cables, not to use new stone.

October 1939 - Air Ministry - Erection and Completion of underground sub-station and incidental works at R.A.F Station Siggiewi (Tas-Salvatur).

The contractor was awarded a contract for soft stone for one year after an invitation for tender that he applied for was accepted in January 1940. The soft stone was to be delivered at sites ordered by' the Admiralty Civil Engineer-in Chiefs-Department delivered at HM. Dockyard and other Naval Establishments around the island. The stone was to be equal in quality to ample submitted market Quality 'A'. The stone had to be sound and free from all defects and roughly squared to the dimension shown in each Order. Delivery was to be made at the place mentioned in each Order within the period stated, and the contractor was required to deliver up to a maximum quantity of 2,500 feet cube per week. Any private lighters or boats which were permitted to berth alongside any Naval Wharf or Jetty were to do so at contractor's risk. The Admiralty was not to accept any liability for damages caused by H.M. Ships or Yard employees. A list extracted from Order Forms for 1940 reveals soft stone delivered in the following locations. In many cases, the order allowed for service transport to be requested to collect the material from the quarry from which the collection was to be made. Also, men entering Armaments Deport were prohibited from taking in any smoking appurtenances.

Work Locations at H.M Dockyard

The following locations in and around the Dockyard area were supplied:

- St. Michael's Bastion, near Senglea School.
- Ghajn Dwieli Gate.

- No2. Generating Station.
- Nos. 4 & 5 Docks.
- Steels Tanks Corradino.
- Marsa A.A. Position.
- Dockyard Telephone Exchange.
- Dockyard North End, Electrical Shop.
- Underground Tanks Corradino.
- Corradino Tunnel.
- H.M.S. St. Angelo.
- No. 1 Dock near Pumping Station.
- No8 M/G House Parlatorio Wharf.
- No 2 Dock East Side.
- Sheer Bastion Refugee.
- Boiler Shop Refugee.
- Victualling Yard.
- Surgery Wharf.
- Canteen Wharf, near O.F. Pipe Tunnel.
- Oil Wharf, Garden Reach.
- Corradino Heights Magazine.

Other Locations:

- Marsascala.
- Dingli Quarters.
- Salini Bay.
- Winch House, Marsamxetto.
- RN. Cemetery.
- RN. Torpedo Depot Msida.
- RN. Hospital.
- RN.Torpedo Depot Kalafrana.
- Petrol Tank, Manoel Island.
- Rifle Range, Ghajn Tuffieha.
- Wireless and Telegraphy Station, Rinella.
- Pinto Stores.
- Naval Armament Depot.
- Salini Bay.
- Construction of Luqa Air Strip.

Contracts Awarded during the Second World War

One of the primary contractors throughout the war was Chev. Angelo Grima. The Directorate of Works of the Air Ministry issued Malta work contracts through a bidding process. These contracts provide insight into the nature, scope, and cost of the work carried out during these pivotal years in Maltese history. The contracts were extremely extensive, with up to 42 clauses covering everything from the scope of the contract to damages, suspension of work, pay, labour during air attacks, and contract termination. The contracts in this section encompass the building of subterranean operating chambers, shelters, stores, hangers, and the removal of rock, stone, soil, and trash, as well as site clearance (Zarb Dimech, 2008).

All of the work had to be done quickly and efficiently, with a control system in place to get the most value out of the limited resources available due to the war effort. In this instance, Angelo Grima of Zejtun, the contractor, obtained supplies from other Maltese enterprises such as Galea Brothers, who were both government and military contractors and located on Blanche Street in Sliema. They were bathroom accessories and fittings importers and sellers and toilets, sinks, closets, and bathtubs. They were also wholesale and retail distributors of contemporary fireplaces, concrete pipes, bannisters, and wall tiling. Items sold to Messrs. Anthony Falzon and Joseph Grima (Angelo's Brother) in May 1940 are included on one of the lists (Zarb Dimech, 2008). These materials were used in work connected with the tenders awarded to the contractor for the following;

- Widening of Roads.
- Underground Operations Chambers.
- Shelters.
- Stores and Hangers.

8/10/1940 -Road Widening:-This contract was awarded for the widening of Kalafrana at Hal Far Road. The work was to be completed within 9 months.

25/2/1941 -Excavating and refilling of Cable Trench (Luqa)- This work was for the excavation and after refilling of cable trench. The work was to be completed on 30/4/1941.

14/3/1941 - Underground Operation Chamber and Shelter (Takali)- An underground Operation Chamber and Shelter at Takali (Torri Cumbo) was awarded for the price of £272, and the completion date was to be 10/6/1941.

The contractor quickly stocked the site with more Maltese miners than were necessary, and he also drove his vehicles to bring the materials. The contractor warned the Air Ministry's Superintending Engineer that it would be difficult to complete the job without interruption on holidays and Sundays, especially given the continuous night blitz. Due to the task's urgency, the contractor also sought the use of impressed lorries and special permissions for them in his letter (Zarb Dimech, 2008).

8/9/1941 - Construction of Underground Hangers and Roads (Luqa) - This contract was for the construction of 6 underground hangers and approach roads at RAF Station Luga, and the price was £18,737.12,6. This was undoubtedly one of the most expensive contracts assigned to a Maltese contractor during the war. The site was handed to the contractor on 14/7/1941, and the work was to be completed on 15/10/1941.

The six underground hangers were tunnelled and excavated at the following rates:

Tunnelling in rock 20/- per cubic yard
Excavating in soil for approaches 3/6 per cubic yard
Excavating in rock for approaches 12/6 per cubic yard

One of the conditions in the contract was that the excavation or tunnelling in rock was to form a segmental underground hangar not exceeding 550 feet super in section and included the levelling of rock floor and trimming rock faces and excavation and all necessary strutting, planking and timbering (Cusens, 2008).

2/12/1941 - Dispersal Points (Hal Far) - This contract was awarded for additional dispersal points and standings at Hal Far Airfield, and the payment was of 3/- per square yard for an area not exceeding 30,000 square yards and 2/9 for areas exceeding 50,000 square yards and not exceeding 50,000 square yards. Work was to be completed on 31/1/1942. Dispersal points and pens were constructed as substantial earth banking with small retaining walls on the inner edges in the rough shape of a letter "E" if viewed from above. These pens offered blast protection for fighter aircraft and their air-crew. Frontpage of Contract (Estimate) for 6 Underground Hangers and Approach Roads (Takali) (Cusens, 2008).

13/1/1942 - Underground Stores (Luqa) - This contract was completed by 15/5/1942 of Underground Stores at Luga RAF Station at the price of £1,778.8.

28/11942 - Underground Shelter (Luqa)

28/11/1942 - Protection for Generator (Takali)

This contract was for the provision of Protected Accommodation for a Generator at Takali at the price of £192 and to be completed on 4/2/1942.

24/5/1942 - Removal of: Rock, Stone, Soil and Rubbish. On or before December 31, 1942, this contract was given to remove rock, stone, spalls, spoil, waste and other materials by carts as and when instructed at all R.A.F installations, with payments provided in accordance with verified carting sheets. For this job, the contractor provided horses and carriages with boxes and the labour needed to load, transport, and stack lumber, as well as a watchman if needed. The work began right away when the contract was signed (Zarb Dimech, 2008).

20/11/1943 - Removal of: Rock, Stone, Soil and Rubbish. Similarly, a contract for Hal Far Aerodrome was set out. A total of 20 horses and carts with boxes (18 cubic feet in size) were agreed upon and another 20 horses and cars with boxes to operate under the control of Officer Commanding 5051 Squadron (Airfield Construction Squadron). The payment was made at a rate of 16 shillings every 8-hour day.

27/9/1941 - Clearing sites (Luqa)- Following an airstrike on Malta's airfields, cleanup work was required. This job entailed cleaning all sandbag blast walls, destroying steelwork corrugated iron, tearing down existing sandbag blast walls and emptying the contents before putting the bags on a roller to combine useable bags.

Unusable bags were to be returned to the Air Ministry Stores with care. The operation also included meticulously gathering all steelwork and corrugated iron from dismantled Bellman Hangars and blots and small components that were to be stored in sandbags. This job was done throughout every available daylight hour, Sundays and holidays included. No portion of the work was to be sublet without the express agreement of the Superintending Engineer (Zarb Dimech, 2008).

Contracts Awarded after Wartime Malta

16/8/44 - H.M. Dockyard -Excavating a trench for electric cable from Lascaris Barracks to Torpedo Deport, Pieta'.

20/12/44- Military -Removal of Cables in Drums and the provision of transport and labour to remove Cables in Drums.

06/12/46 – Military -The provision of transport and labour for the removal of cables in drums for the period from 01/01/47 to 30/6/47.

The Royal Army Service Corps requested the contractor on 16 October 1945 to move cable drums as follows:

- 2 from Msida to Great Siege Road weighting approximately 2 and half tons each.
- 1 from Fort St. Rocco to Great Siege Road, weighing 1 ton.
- 2 from Fort Leonardo to Great Siege Road, weighing 1 and a half tons each.

On 15 September 1945, 3 drums of cable were unloaded from H.M.S Weavely.

The above are only a few examples of the many movements of cable drums. Cable drums were also taken to the cable dump, where the cable drums were stacked. The contractor complained in May 1945 about the dump's very poor state, especially where heavy transport is concerned. After the war, through a letter dated 28 February 1944, the Wing Commander Superintending Engineer informed the contractor that under the contracts of 1943, horses and cars supplied under these contracts were to terminate from February 1944 (Zarb Dimech, 2008).

Claims for Losses

Because they were the launching pad for the Allied air force, the RAF stations were the target of intense Axis strikes on Malta. During the second and third weeks of March 1942, air raids on airfields occurred at all hours of the day and night. Airfields resembled lunar landscapes, and the civilian population was also affected by the carpet bombing. Due to the airstrikes, Maltese contractors could not complete their job by the agreed-upon time (Zarb Dimech, 2008).

Angelo Grima, the contractor, demanded reimbursement for the lost time. One of the conditions that the contractor had to comply with was that by 9:00 am the day following an air raid; he had to deliver a return of all the working time lost during the air raids when the stoppage of work occurred, names of workmen on the job, rates of wages (Zarb Dimech, 2008).

A particular contract referred to a contract of work at Wied Dalam on which the Air Ministry paid compensation. However, the contractor complained that his claims for this extra cost had not been paid on many of his wartime contracts. He also stated that the amount was very considerable in sum and, in many cases, meant the difference between loss and recovery of his costs on some of his contracts. During the intense air raids and the subsequent siege of Malta, the men had much less vitality than normal, and in consequence, their output suffered due to the following reasons (Zarb Dimech, 2008):

- Lack of food due to Siege Conditions.
- Continual air raids, especially at night, causing loss of sleep and general deterioration of vitality.
- Air raids occurring during transit to and from work.

Time lost during these raids was paid at the daily rate, and no deduction was made if they were late due to an air raid while on the way to work. Up to the period in 1941, local regulations were that all traffic must stop between the 'air raid warning' and the 'all clear".

The advent of hostilities in Malta made the construction of underground shelters of paramount importance, and miners were in great demand. They were thus able to earn wages above normal, and many of the best men left to take advantage of the higher wages. Many men not previously classed as miners had to be employed, and they were not up to the stand of a normal miner.

Inferior quality and scarcity of materials of gunpowder, coal of blacksmiths forge to sharpen tools, bad lighting etc. According to the contractor, the above causes began about 3 months after the commencement of hostilities in Malta (beginning of September 1940 until the end of the contract).

The work was carried out under the threat of aerial bombardment, and sometimes work had to be stopped because of the need for the workers to take cover, yet making sure that on completion of the work they would be reimbursed of their expenditure and derive some profit from their labours.

The following is a list of services and stations that the Contractor, Angelo Grima, was awarded between 1941 and 1943, on which he presented claims for losses sustained due to war conditions:

Station Service

Takali (Excavation of Underground Shelter)
Luqa (Removal of 3000 Drums of Tar, etc.)

Takali (Underground Hangars 1-6)
Luqa (Clearing Sites)
MXlokk (Barrack Accommodation)
Hal Far (Road Taxi Strip)
TaKali (Protected Access to Generator)
TaKali (4 Underground Shelters)
Hal Far (Dispersal and Hard-Standings)
Luqa (Underground Stores)
Luqa (Underground Shelter)
Hal Far (Perimeter Track and Links)
Luqa (Torpedo Store)
Valletta (Provision of Day Labour)
Valletta (Carting)
Wied Dalam (Barrack Block etc.)
All Stations (Supply of Horses and Carts)
Wied Dalam (Delivery of Spalls)
Wied Dalam (S/O Hardstone Spalls)
Siggiewi (Cable Trench)
Hal Far (Horses and Carts)
Hal Far (Road Widening etc.)
Hal Far (Road Widening)
Luqa (Cable Trench)
Luga (Underground Bomb Stores)
Takali (Underground Operation Chamber)
Wied Dalam (Ventilating Shaft)
Marsa (Repairs to Command Petrol Pool)

This list of claims by Angelo Grima was submitted to the Under Secretary of State, Air Ministry in a detailed document dated 24th April 1942, and this sheds light on the tools, sources of energy required for the work and the war conditions prevailing during the contractor's work. Keeping in mind that conditions in Malta differed considerably from those prevailing in England where rates of wages, materials, etc., were controlled, wage rates in Malta increased from July 1940 at varying periods. The contractor was obliged to pay equal rates to those paid by other contractors, particularly the Shelter Construction Department, to retain men. The contract rates were based upon the output capacity of men who had worked for the contractor for several years and amongst whom were some of the best miners on the Island. When the Shelter Construction Department offered substantially higher wages, the contractor lost many of these men and was obliged to employ inexperienced men who needed constant supervision. The contractor had to pay an additional 5/- per day each to four of his best men to supervise and motivate these men. Without this extra supervision, the contractor would not have been able to maintain progress.

Chapter 8

Key Characteristics and Themes

Data collecting is an important aspect of every study. Data makes it easy to assess a situation and determine why particular actions and decisions were made and the underlying structure of a study. The writers of this book collect data to comprehend the context of the building work done during the war, to understand the thinking behind decisions made, and pave the way for new ideas and prospects in post-war strategy.

Data Collection Overview

The key thematic elements of a generic framework to guide the research in identifying contractual arrangements were explored through a literature review that examined responses to externally initiated rapid change. A historical review of the development of construction in Malta during the war was then undertaken by examining the social needs, the environment, and the profiles of the key individuals involved. That is the background and drive that people (especially the main character) had to identify, seek and realise opportunities.

A literature list was compiled, including a historical background of people, the general functioning of the Maltese islands at the time, the impact of the war on Malta, the Maltese construction industry, and the contractual arrangements made. This provided the necessary background knowledge for the book. As the management of environmental disasters in terms of applying contingency methods to manage change was a new area of research, the authors conducted a thematic analysis to identify the critical issues using the data collected, key findings and case study material.

The authors identified this as a response to crises in construction and sought to understand how it worked and how it could be applied to day-to-day management. The theoretical framework developed from the data addressed the following: the resource capacity and resilience within which the book's main character operated; the structures required to facilitate the response; the operating environment, informed by elements of the crisis and complexity; the key elements maintaining service continuity in the sector.

Data analysis began and occurred alongside the interview collection process from which data was drawn. Data analysis required a constant shift between immersion, coding, categorising and creating themes (Green et al., 2007). To systematically make sense of the entire data set, the authors repeatedly practised the process described above. The analytical process needed to be constantly 'testing the fit' as new data was integrated into the analysis (Green et al., 2007). The conceptual and theoretical framework also structured the study design and influenced the process of sampling and data collection. During data collection in this book, detailed reports on each topic were produced in the interview studies and in analysing the interview data, the authors cite Rapley (2004), who states that "you should analyse what actually happened, how your interaction produced that trajectory of talk, how specific versions of reality are co-constructed, how specific identities, discourses, and narratives are produced".

Thematic saturation was achieved when further observation and analysis yielded no more new topics. As was the case in this research, saturation can be reached without discovering the fullness of relationships between themes (Glaser and Strauss, 2009). In most cases, there was no direct relationship between themes, but data saturation sought to support the research conclusions, as is common in many qualitative sampling methods (usually non-probabilistic and purposive). This application of saturation is intended to answer the question, "Are the observations sufficient to justify the claims and conclusions?", thus guiding the authors to complete, continue sampling or refine their sampling methodology to fill in gaps (in theory) that appeared to have low saturation (Glaser and Strauss, 2009).

Case Study Strategy

The data collection techniques used in this book included interviews, observation, and document analysis (Saunders et al., 2007). Case study strategies require authors and researchers to triangulate multiple data sources. Yin (2003) distinguishes between four case study strategies, including single or multiple, holistic or embedded studies. The scope of a case study is to investigate a contemporary phenomenon within its real-life context, especially when the boundaries between phenomenon and context are not evident.' (Yin 2003, p. 13) A case study 'tries to illuminate a *decision* or set of decisions:

why they were taken, how they were implemented, and with what result.' (Schramm, 1971 cited in Yin, 2003, p. 12) Saunders *et al.* (2007) sustain that a case study strategy is useful when researchers need to gain a rich understanding of the context of the research and the processes being enacted. This book addresses how the engagement of public contracts allowed the managerial activity to take place as a response to environmental change.

The case study method refers to the development of detailed intensive knowledge about a single 'case' or a small number of related 'cases' (Robson, 1993). The rationale for using a single case study is when it represents a critical case in testing a well-formulated theory or when the case is unique or an extreme (Yin, 2003). Using two or more cases produces stronger results, with complementary or contrasting strategies followed by analytic conclusions, which are more powerful than conclusions arising from one (Yin, 2003). In this book, the multiple cases of construction contracts were considered more effective than a single case study. The rationale for using multiple cases relates to the need to establish whether the findings of the first case occurred in other cases and, consequently, generalise from these findings (Saunders et al., 2007).

For the authors of this book, the closeness of the case study to real-life situations and its varied richness of detail was important in two ways: the development of a nuanced view of reality and the importance of research case studies for researchers' learning processes in developing skills (Flyvbjerg, 2006). Furthermore, Flyvbjerg (2006) points out that generalisation based on a single case is possible, depending on the case one is talking about and how it is chosen. This applies to both the natural sciences and the study of human affairs.

The main aim of this case study research was to use in-depth interviews to focus on obtaining rich and detailed information. Healy and Perry's (2000) six specific criteria for assessing the validity and reliability of case studies is one such method to explore this within the realism paradigm. The authors were clear that using a case study method for theory building was based on the need to understand real-life phenomena and gain new holistic and in-depth insights, explanations, and interpretations about the rich experiences of previously unknown practitioners. The authors were aware that they had to refrain from making subjective judgements during the research design and data collection to enhance construct validity (Riege, 2003). In this case study research, internal validity required credible ascertainment of phenomena, which was accomplished through interviews, observation, and document analysis. Case study research specifically aims to find generative mechanisms that allow inferences about real-life experiences. In this case, the authors highlight the main emergent components of the interviewees' experiences and determine which components are significant for the patterns studied and which mechanisms generated them (Riege, 2003). External validity was concerned with extrapolating particular research findings beyond the immediate form of the study. Reliability was achieved by ensuring that the process of data collection, *i.e.,* the procedures and practises of the study, could be repeated by other researchers to produce similar results, i.e., the extent of the findings could be replicated, provided that, for example, the interview techniques and procedures remained the same (Riege, 2003).

Identifying the Main Drivers to seek opportunities in a time of distress, high unemployment, hunger, no income, and low morale meant conquering the crisis of time to generate more opportunities. The main character in this novel had to push beyond the ordinary. A strong desire to succeed is at the heart of every successful endeavour. If one wants to take an opportunity in the face of hardship, there is a means to mastering adversity.

The following main drivers were identified in this context:

Asking for Help

Chev. Grima, the book's main character, takes the initiative to ask his unemployed clients if they would be interested in a job offer. When asking for help, first and foremost, understand what your need is and how you can solve or address it. When you do, you encourage others to join your cause, which has the added benefit of building resources to find a solution. In a time when morale was down, the main character managed to overcome that downfall and pool talents to support a common cause.

Participation

Angelo was given the contract, and all of the workers worked and were paid, so he made a profit. This was the start of his career as a contractor, and it was a humble beginning. Finding the proper opportunity at the right moment provides assurance, which allows for new ideas and creative possibilities for everyone involved. Knowing how to seek opportunities and where to look for them offers you an advantage over others who do not. Building relationships with individuals who can give the appropriate connections and opportunities at the right moment is crucial to participation.

Intuition/Spirituality

Refers to being in tune with the needs of the times and seeking supernatural guidance. The main character in this book was a man with a deep spiritual conviction and mystical guidance that he found necessary to participate in many strategic decisions to protect his workforce and operate safely in a time of distress. Understanding something that went beyond the mind and involved the supernatural helped guide many ventures through a safe passage.

Risk-Taking

Angelo contributed to family responsibilities, public projects, educational assistance, and, among other things, the founding of Malta's first airline. He was very private about his humanitarian acts, building houses for clergy, helping numerous families on the verge of destitution, and keeping his fortune hidden. The element of risk was always present, and his response to risk meant reacting to the permutations and combinations of events as they occurred through time. The plans formed and the judgments made, particularly by people with power, have a significant impact on how quickly danger may be eradicated from a community, and, in this situation, one character accepted a huge risk to rescue the lives of others.

Malta experienced difficult times as it tried to rebuild itself architecturally, spiritually, and economically. With the aftermath of the war still being felt for several years after it ended, fear and suffering became ingrained in Maltese culture, and unfortunately, it took many years to wash away from the nation's subconscious, as the struggle for resources ramified. Despite these times, there have always been people in history who have overcome adversity and set new standards by helping others along the way. True leadership is shown by those who are willing to give and who, when things get tough, stand up and give more rather than retreat. War conditions require endurance and perseverance, apart from the mental capacity to live in uncertainty for a long period. Coming to terms with loss and understanding how this character responded, how he engaged in the world, how he faced challenges optimistically, and how he overcame trauma is one way to write about how people can improve their lives and the lives of others.

Sustainability

While conflict might divert resources away from more critical issues, Angelo's ideas and methods preserved continuity and did not jeopardize future generations' needs. Angelo's dreams, in reality, lived on via his brothers, the workers, and their offspring for many years after his death. Angelo was aware of the present requirements, but he saw that thinking the same way would provide the same old outcomes. Risks change throughout time and should not be managed in the same way. He saw the need for contracts, a passenger airline, and a resting house for retired clergy, which he founded with his brothers. The latter is a challenge that many countries have yet to overcome. Sustainability aims to ensure that we preserve our natural systems' ability to produce the natural resources and ecosystem services that we need. However, if we are just concerned with the 'feel good' component of the moment, we are disconnected from future demands, which leads us to eradicate and utilize whatever is required to get by in the present.

Closure

The organisation of the war effort under war conditions in Malta is remarkable, and it is of great merit for Malta being the most bombed place on earth. It was also one of the most organised civil societies after Britain during World War II. This organisation was visible regarding the civil aspect of defence in areas such as Air Raid Precautions, evacuation, shelter excavation, demolition and clearance and others, but also in the building, maintenance and supply of strategic military, naval and air force installations around the island.

The writers could not help but appreciate the effectiveness, efficiency, and productivity of the British soldiers and the Maltese contractor and his staff while producing this book, which was based mostly on records from Contractor Angelo Grima. Under the disciplined guidance of Maltese and British commanders, the contractor's personnel, mules, carts, lorries, and raw supplies permitted a collaborative effort in which all the know-how and skills were pooled together. The result is an astonishing amount of work completed in a short period by Maltese employees at the H.M Dockyard, R.N. bases, airfields, and other infrastructure supporting Malta's defence before, during, and after WWII. Despite the overall difficulties that the situations presented, the success of the work effort is underlined all along in this research.

Malta was truly a 'thorn in the enemy's side' and an 'unsinkable aircraft carrier that contributed greatly to the Axis forces' downfall. Although the study is not exhaustive, further studies on this topic may be a suggested course of action for other authors to explore in greater depth for one of the most glorious chapters in Maltese construction history.

What Does It Take to Identify Opportunities and Act on Them?

Understanding the Skillsets of the Workforce

Identifying skills and matching the work needed with the skillsets available at the time was a key element in identifying opportunities, and the key roles in the book were able to take advantage of such a situation. To recognise an opportunity in a business is to understand what that business could benefit from in a time of need. At the beginning of the book, it was clear how contracting Maltese workers and Maltese companies revitalised the island through labour. To achieve this, it was necessary to resort to new opportunities from which these resources could be drawn in a time of scarcity. Moreover, much of Malta's infrastructure was badly damaged after the war, so teaching people how to be economical with materials and time was crucial for quickly responding to emergencies and building.

One may occasionally see abandoned sites that never received post-war upkeep on the island, resulting in neglect and regular vandalism. Those with a keen eye for renovation, on the other hand, are aware of how a revitalized neighbourhood may benefit a city's economy. This must be done in tandem with training people how to recognize and respond to possibilities - the skill of converting a mundane product into something extraordinary. Art and architecture require supervision and instruction, and, like the major people in this story, the key to success has always been the benign urge to share the fruits of one's labour.

A Focus on Profit for Purpose

One of the most important aspects of any company plan is to generate a profit. As previously stated in previous chapters, the main character prioritized 'purpose' over profit margin, which led to growth as a direct result of diversifying his portfolio. Putting others first is consistent with the Golden Rule, which is found in Luke 6:31: 'Do unto others as you would have them do unto you.' In contrast to many traditional company strategies that are only focused on profit, the application of the Golden Rule in this case study appeared to satisfy the greater framework of addressing needs by assuring a benefit for all or most community members, sometimes known as the 'common good.' According to Aristotle, St. Thomas Aquinas, John Locke, David Hume, and Jean-Jacques Rousseau, the' common good, ' to mention a few, is the purpose of the universal will and the highest goal to be pursued by the government. When times are tough due to tight schedules or low profitability, we may be inclined to cut down on something beneficial. For example, a reduction in worker compensation or even layoffs. Nonetheless, it appeared that the main character understood the concept of 'common good' early on in his career. When the company made decisions based on values, the results were dependent not only on the economic drivers of the time but also on the understanding that the main function was to provide a service for a strong community, and adherence to this principle seemed to have crystallized clearly in this case.

How Does One Realise the Opportunity and Finance It?

The case study demonstrated that timing of opportunity is one of the fundamental parts of anything that succeeds since the gap formed is filled by a timely chance to work. The recognition of the right timing to work means that response can happen as the need arises. Perseverance is a second important factor since a combination of risk and sustained achievement was needed to ensure that one job led to another, and so on. Thirdly, because a seed investor was working on behalf of a community, an opportunity for the community was created. This, coupled with a leading, dominant role, is crucial for fulfilling any opportunity. When an opportunity is identified, and someone is willing to capitalize on it, the door is opened for it to begin. Working in construction is a complicated and sometimes tough endeavour that takes a plethora of parts to come together to make it function, so in a manner, it pushed for a new age in construction prospects to a rising section of society. With the economy's strength being linked to building activity, it functioned as a method for reviving Malta during the time.

Construction is an essential component of every country's growth. This case study highlighted that as work progressed, a ripple of change happened, suggesting that there must be a strong sector within which to operate for an opportunity to take off. A robust trade allows for expansion, sometimes known as a 'cash cow' in a company, potentially growing if profit stability is reached. In this regard, the sector was strong, and the product was effective. Thus, any further lessons learned from this may be summarized as follows: timing and capitalising on opportunity, strong leadership, and selection of a strong sector within which to operate. Suppose you have an idea, but no money, and an investor has money and the need but no idea. How can the idea get off the ground, and how can it be financed? As long as one can meet the two needs, financing becomes possible.

Angelo might have had to drop out of school at an early stage. This might have limited his skills. However, he proved himself a visionary who observed and viewed things from a perspective that others might not have had the ability, attitude, determination and energy to make a difference and challenge the status quo. This inner strength and ability might have resulted from the responsibility and hardship he had to face at a young age to take care of his younger siblings. He viewed the hardship of the time as an opportunity, and a means to ensure sustainability for the people of his town and his family.

He observed and understood that if these people joined strengths and abilities, they could tender for the construction requirements brought about by the war. He managed to create a chain of material suppliers and labourers to meet the demands of the time, helping to feed many families who depended on this chain of contracts.

Experience of hardship at a young age, belief in the providence of God and that God will give him the ability and skills to succeed, trust in the people and them in him, and a positive attitude and determination were key to sourcing the demand and finance.

In summary, Angelo had good observation, communication and negotiating skills. He knew how to marry the chain of needs to deliver objectives. It is a journey, which is constantly marked by the following sentiments in a family's trust and dialogue with God: "I tasted you, and now hunger and thirst for you; you touched me, and I have burned for your peace." (St Augustine, Confessions X, XXVII, 38.)

Resource Management

The resources to which underprivileged citizens have limited or no access cripples the nature of prosperity. The laws of nature have a say when it comes to the distribution of wealth, but other laws that may not be discussed in usual circles are laws of power, such as the Pareto principle, which states that 80% of the effects come from the 20% of the causes, which determines the distribution of power and its influence on all global transactions. The allocation of power in the Bible is different. The famous *Last Supper Act* is a culminating symbol of wealth distribution – one that was entirely based on an action of sharing of oneself and one's destiny to the death penalty. One might add that sharing *a last supper* act would influence many prestigious artists to depict this historic moment in time for decades to come. The historical advantages left by significant persons in history who sat with the destitute and hungry to share all that was theirs differed from those left by emperors, kingdoms, and prosperous civilizations, not in terms of power but in terms of resource distribution.

The principle of 'what is mine, is yours' also used in marriage ceremonies is a symbolism that can only be understood when the nature or cycle of abuse is broken, which hinders the true meaning of this principle. A common deception of *being used* by someone (or an entity) is the painful root of blocking the freedom and security to give to others. Citing yet again Proverbs 11:24-25, we can understand this further through the following, 'One gives freely yet grows all the richer; another withholds what he should give and only suffers want. Whoever brings blessing will be enriched, and one who waters will himself be watered.'

The poverty mindset is an attitude founded upon the perception of lack and adopted by those who experience insufficiency, recognises that wealth can be difficult to share, and survival is through collection or hoarding even when sufficiency is reached. The absence of a spirit of freedom in giving and receiving is also a principle that is subject to natural law and must be practised in different ways. Alternatively, we may find ourselves in a position where we cannot accept the gift of financial help. This means that poverty thinking is still in play but hinders economic recovery because of other underlying principles: shame, guilt, helplessness, or self-pity. On the other hand, wealthy populations can be characterised by a poverty mentality because they cannot see that the wealth that has been accumulated is enough for them, so they are in a constant cycle of enrichment that is strictly about "getting more". This is also poverty thinking.

Communities and institutions function best when people's perspectives are focused on sharing and equitable resource distribution to balance out disparities across factions. Throughout the book, the theme is one of continual support for the weaker in a post-war period when the general thinking mindset would be inclined towards the reverse. This would allow the reader to determine whether this style of doing things is close or far from their basic belief system. During times of economic austerity, we are provided with an example of an entrepreneur who treated the disadvantaged as an extension of his family. This is something that is of major concern on a worldwide basis in terms of the educative direction taken when discussing universal wealth and its distribution across nations. When studying financial wealth management and its application to global resources, we must be aware of the impact that international financial decisions may have on meeting the needs of the vulnerable, or better still, the potential that lies ahead if key decision-takers act as a catalyst for the creation of equality as opposed to dysfunctionality.

Human Vulnerability

We have prioritised a global system management over our immediate health needs. The economic decisions being made are designed to meet this higher demand, but they cripple their users in the process. The way towards new progress is to step outside the global management construct and encourage people to initiate small management circles, particularly the vulnerable and underprivileged, to benefit from the miracles of management. We have seen death in all circles of society after the war, so even wealth cannot stop the principle of death. Overusing our resources and their limits and before their time is a war on humanity, and along with changing climatic circumstances, needs a new approach to resource management.

Resource management is a way of life since it is linked to a sustainable lifestyle. We choose our decisions about what to consume, how much to consume, and how much waste we choose to create. On the other hand, if we consider this from a policy perspective, resource management necessitates suitable process routes that are not bureaucratically inhibited, particularly when one nation wants to transfer life support systems (food, water, medications, and so on) to another country. Management must be transparent, and we must recognize that our transactions must be regulated for acceptable systems to operate. A large cultural attitude has to be explored - the huge argument about why current trends in resource management lean toward the use and discard culture, which leads to waste and poisoning life, leaving us to bear the consequences of our overly wasteful habits. As a result of capitalism, society has come to believe that this is yours and this is mine; rather than let us share what we have. We must recognize that this will have to alter shortly because everything on earth is finite.

Most significantly, and as the last addition to this book, we feel that one cannot share with another person until we first comprehend that we are "one" - a concept that, as this book has demonstrated, has enormous potential if allowed to pervade families and their cultures. However, it might also be imposed on us because of natural phenomena which can shock humanity to a new state of being. If not, nature itself will force us to act in unity, soon, as we face change.

References

Anckar, D. (2004). "Regime choices in microstates: the cultural constraint", *Commonwealth and Comparative Politics*, Vol. 42 No. 2, pp. 206-223.

Bezzina, F., Grima, S., & Mamo, J., (2014). Risk Management practices adopted by financial firms in Malta, *Managerial Finance*, (Emerald Group Publishing Ltd.) vol. 40, no. 6, pp 587-612.

Blouet, B.W. (2004). *The Story of Malta,* Malta: Progress Press Co Ltd.

Bondin, R. (2014). 1979: end of 449 years of Malta as a military base. *Times of Malta*. [ONLINE] Available at: https://timesofmalta.com/articles/view/1979-end-of-449-years-of-malta-as-a-military-base.512742 [Accessed 2 October 2021].

Bishop A. (n.d.) *Underground life during the war: Malta's air-raid shelters.* [ONLINE] Available at: https://www.guidememalta.com/en/underground-life-during-the-war-malta-s-air-raid-shelters [Accessed 2 October 2021].

Clark G.E. (2008). War and Sustainability: The Economic and Environmental Costs, *Environment: Science and Policy for Sustainable Development,* 50:1, 3-4, DOI: 10.3200/ENVT.50.1.3-5.

Church Fathers (1887). *The Confessions* (Book X) St. Augustine. https://www.newadvent.org/fathers/110110.htm.

Cusens, S. (2008). *Maltese Construction work at RAF stations in Malta during WWII* [ONLINE] Available at: https://www.independent.com.mt/articles/2008-06-08/local-news/Maltese-Construction-work-at-RAF-stations-in-Malta-during-WWII-208712 [Accessed 2 October 2021].

Dulles, E. (1942). War and Investment Opportunities: An Historical Analysis. *The American Economic Review, 32*(1), 112–128.

Glaser, B.G., Strauss, A.L. (2009). *The discovery of grounded theory: Strategies for qualitative research, 4th* ed. New Brunswick, NJ: Aldine.

Green, J., Willis, K., Hughes, E., Small, R., Welch, N., Gibbs, L. and Daly, J. (2007), Generating best evidence from qualitative research: the role of data analysis. *Australian and New Zealand Journal of Public Health,* 31: 545-550. https://doi-org.ejournals.um.edu.mt/10.1111/j.1753-6405.2007.00141.x.

Grima, S., Dalli Gonzi, R., Thalassinos, E. 2020. The Impact of COVID-19 on Malta and its Economy and Sustainable Strategies. *The Journal of Corporate Governance, Insurance, and Risk Management* (JCGIRM). 2020, Volume 7, Series 1. pp53-73.

Grima, S., Hamarat, B., Özen, E., Girlando, A. and Dalli-Gonzi, R. (2021). The Relationship between Risk Perception and Risk Definition and Risk-Addressing Behaviour during the Early COVID-19 Stages. *Journal of Risk and Financial Management* 14: 272.https://doi.org/10.3390/jrfm14060272.

Hart, O. (2001). "Financial Contracting." *Journal of Economic Literature* 39 (4): 1079–1100. https://doi.org/10.1257/jel.39.4.1079.

Healy, M. and Perry, C. (2000). 'Comprehensive criteria to judge validity and reliability of qualitative research within the realism paradigm', *Qualitative Market Research: An International Journal,* Vol. 3 No. 3, pp. 118-26.

Nora Boustany (2001). "The Consummate Diplomat Wants Malta on the Map". *The Washington Post.* Retrieved 6 July 2017.

Pirotta, G.A. (2001). "A new creation or an image and likeliness? The Maltese experience of establishing a local government in a centralised micro-state", *Public Organization Review: A Global Journal,* Vol. 1 No. 2, pp. 245-260.

Rapley, T. (2004). Interviews. In: Seale C, Gobo G, Gubrium J, Silverman D, editor. *Qualitative Research Practice.* London (UK): Sage. p. 15– 33.

Riege, A.M. (2003). Validity and reliability tests in case study research: A literature review with "hands-on" applications for each research phase. *Qualitative Market Research.* 26(2):75-86.

Samy, Y., Carment, D., Prest, S and Gagne′, J.F. (2008). "Small states, resilience and governance", in Briguglio, L., Cordina, G., Farrugia, N. and Vigilance, C. (Eds), *Small States and the Pillars of Economic Resilience*, (pp. 217-242). Msida: University of Malta. Islands and Small States Institute & London: The Commonwealth Secretariat.

Spooner, Tony (1996). *Supreme Gallantry: Malta's Role in the Allied Victory, 1939–1945*. London. ISBN 978-0719557064.

Taylor, A.J.P. (1974). Mayer, S.L. (ed.). *A History Of World War Two.* London: Octopus Books. ISBN 0-7064-0399-1.

The World Bank (2013). *"Worldwide governance indicators",* [ONLINE] Available at: http://info.worldbank.org/governance/wgi/index.aspx#reports [Accessed 2 October 2021].

Vernd, E. (2003). *Architectural theory: from the Renaissance to the present.* Taschen P.845. ISBN 978-3-8228-1699-8.

Wiest, J.B. (2013). My Wartime Self: Meaning Construction in Narratives of World War II. *Narrative Works*, *3*(1). [ONLINE] Available at: https://journals.lib.unb.ca/index.php/NW/article/view/21066 [Accessed 2 October 2021]

Zarb -Dimech, A. (2002). *Taking Cover, A History of Air Raid Shelters:* Malta 1940-43

Zarb-Dimech, A. (2008) *Maltese Construction work at RAF Stations in Malta during WWII.* [ONLINE] Available at: https://www.independent.com.mt/articles/2008-06-08/local-news/Maltese-Construction-work-at-RAF-stations-in-Malta-during-WWII-208712 [Accessed 1 May 2022]

Zarb -Dimech, A. (2010). *A Maltese Personality from Zejtun: Chevalier Angelo Grima.* (Is-Sur Gulin tal-Qutu). [ONLINE] Available at: https://www.independent.com.mt/articles/2010-04-24/news/a-maltese-personality-from-zejtun-chevalier-angelo-grima-is-sur-gulin-tal-qutu-273569 [Accessed 2 October 2021]

Zarb-Dimech, A. (2011) *Animal Transport in Malta for the British Military* (1930-1942) [ONLINE]Available at: https://www.independent.com.mt/articles/2011-08-28/local-news/Animal-Transport-in-Malta-for-the-British-Military-(1930-1942)-297741 [Accessed 1 May 2022]

Newspapers and Other References

After the Battle Magazine/Issue 10/MALTA G.C./WW2 era/54 pages/1975.

Air Ministry. (1948). *The Rise and Fall of the German Air Force 1933- 1945.* St Martin's Press.

Aquilina J. (1987). *Maltese-English Dictionary.* Midsea Books Ltd.

Bezzina, C. (2004). *The Gozo Airfield.* Gozo: J. Debono Printing Press.

Blouet, B. (2004). *The story of Malta.* Progress Press Co Ltd.

Chisholm, Hugh, ed. (1911). "Barocchio, Giacomo". *Encyclopedia Britannica.* Vol. 3 (11th ed.). Cambridge University Press. p. 417.

Corriere Della Sera, Friday 28 June 1940.

Fenech, N. (2007). *Richard Ellis, The Photography Collection, Valletta & Floriana.* Book Distributors (BDL) Limited.

Galea, F. (2002). *Call-Out, a wartime diary of air/sea rescue operation at Malta.* Malta at War Publications.

Harrison, A. St. B. & Hubbard. R.P.S. (1945). *Valletta and Three Cities, A Report to accompany the Outline Plan for the Region of Valletta and the Three Cities, prepared for the Government of Malta.* Government of Malta.

Holland, James (2003). *Fortress Malta: An Island Under Siege, 1940–1943.* London: Miramax Books. ISBN 1-4013-5186-7.

Maltese War Propaganda Leaflets, Lupi Press.

Manson J.L. (1945). *Experimental Building Science*, Vol. I, Introduction to Science as Applied in Building, Cambridge University Press.

National War Association Photos

Pace, R. (2009). The Gozo Airfield. – Eisenhower's Recollections. *The Gozo Observer* (No.21) December.

RAF Contracts and documents of Angelo Grima Admirality and Naval Contractor.

Spetiz A.R. (1910). *The Styles of Ornament* (Ed. R. Phene Spiers).

Sunday Circle of November 2009 issued with Sunday Times of Malta.

The Official History of New Zealand in the Second World War 1939–1945 | NZETC. (2016). *Official History of New Zealand in the Second World War.* [ONLINE] Available at: http://nzetc.victoria.ac.nz/tm/scholarly/tei-corpus-WH2.html [Accessed 01 January 2022].

Zammit V., Cilia D. (2004) *The Limestone Heritage: Siggiewi.* Heritage Books.

Photographs

Abela A. (1942). *3LAA Regiment, Royal Malta Artillery.*

Bishop, A. (n.d.) *Underground life during the war: Malta's air-raid shelters. [ONLINE]* Available at: https://www.guidememalta.com/en/underground-life-during-the-war-malta-s-air-raid-shelters [Accessed 01 January 2022].

Ellis F.L. (n.d.). *pre-1950s photos of Malta showing what life was like back then.* [ONLINE] Available at: https://www.guidememalta.com/en/13-pre-1950s-photos-of-malta-showing-what-life-was-like-back-then. [Accessed 01 January 2022].

Armoured Aircraft Carriers in World War II. (2022). *Armoured Aircraft Carriers.* [ONLINE] Available at: https://www.armouredcarriers.com/illustrious-blitz-january-12-21. [Accessed 01 January 2022].

Harrison A.S.B. & Hunnard R.P.S., (1945) *Valletta and Three Cities, A Report to accompany the outline plan for the region of Valetta and the Three Cities.* Valletta: Government of Malta.

Malta at War (Magazine) by Richard Mifsud, 1975.

Malta360. (n.d.) *Map of the Cottonera and Santa Margherita Lines.* Available at: https://maltain360.com/default.aspx.

Maltese History & Heritage. (n.d.) *Fortifications | Maltese History & Heritage.* [ONLINE] Available at: https://vassallohistory.wordpress.com/fortifications/. [Accessed 01 January 2022].

Mizzi J.A., Vella M.A. (2001). *Malta at War.* Malta: Wise Owl.

Reemt Peters-Hein, R. (n.d.). *The radar station at the Dingli Cliffs, Malta.* [ONLINE] Available at: https://www.locationscout.net/malta/4723-radar-station-at-the-dingli-cliffs. [Accessed 01 January 2022].

Russell, J.E. (Lt) (n.d.) *Extensive bomb damage in Valletta, 1942*. [ONLINE] Available at: http://media.iwm.org.uk/iwm/mediaLib//29/media-29365/large.jpg [Accessed 01 January 2022].

The National Archives of Malta (n.d.). *Wied Dalam.* [ONLINE] Available at https://arkivji.org.mt/share/Plans/PDM61411.jpg [Accessed 01 January 2022].

Times of Malta. (2022). *Key positions: Malta's World War II radars.* [ONLINE] Available at: https://timesofmalta.com/articles/view/key-positions-maltas-world-war-ii-radars.651667. [Accessed 01 January 2022]

Vanderveen, B. (1930). *Historic Military Vehicles Directory,* Poland: After the Battle Publication.

Authors' Contact Information

Dr. Rebecca Dalli Gonzi
Construction & Property Management Department, Faculty for the Built Environment, University of Malta
rebecca.e.dalli-gonzi@um.edu.mt

Prof. Simon Grima
Department of Insurance and Risk Management, Faculty of Economics, Management and Accountancy, University of Malta.
simon.grima@um.edu.mt

Anthony Zarb Dimech
Freelance Researcher and Writer
anthonyzd7@gmail.com

Index